No Choice but to Follow

linked poems by
Jean Yamasaki Toyama | Juliet S. Kono
Ann Inoshita | Christy Passion

Bamboo Ridge Press

ISBN 978-0-910043-82-3

This is issue #96 (Fall 2009) of *Bamboo Ridge, Journal of Hawaiʻi Literature and Arts* (ISSN 0733-0308).

Text and CD copyright © 2010 by Bamboo Ridge Press

All rights reserved. This book, or parts thereof, may not be reproduced in any form without permission.

Published by Bamboo Ridge Press

Printed in the United States of America

Indexed in the Humanities International Complete

Bamboo Ridge Press is a member of the Council of Literary Magazines and Presses (CLMP).

Typesetting and design: Rowen Tabusa

Cover art: "Stray Dog," 2008, by Russell Sunabe, oil on canvas, 39.5" H X 32.75" W.

Authors' photos by Rowen Tabusa

Audio CD recorded in the Atherton Studio of Hawaii Public Radio.
    Sammie Choy, producer
    Jason Taglianetti, engineer

Bamboo Ridge Press is a nonprofit, tax-exempt corporation formed in 1978 to foster the appreciation, understanding, and creation of literary, visual, or performing arts by, for, or about Hawaiʻi's people. This project was supported in part by grants from the National Endowment for the Arts (NEA) and the Hawaiʻi State Foundation on Culture and the Arts (SFCA), celebrating more than forty years of culture and the arts in Hawaiʻi. The SFCA is funded by appropriations from the Hawaiʻi State Legislature and by grants from the NEA. Funding was also provided by the University of Hawaiʻi Office of Student Equity, Excellence and Diversity (SEED) and the Hawaiʻi Council for the Humanities, with additional support from the "We the People" initiative of the National Endowment for the Humanities.

Bamboo Ridge is published twice a year. For subscription information, back issues, or a catalog, please contact:

    Bamboo Ridge Press; P.O. Box 61781; Honolulu, HI 96839-1781
    (808) 626-1481; brinfo@bambooridge.com
    www.bambooridge.com

5 4 3 2 1   10 11 12 13 14

This collection of linked *renshi* poems has much heart, delicacy and interconnectedness on personal and social levels in Hawai'i and beyond, so it is a fitting 30th anniversary commemoration for the wonderful work of *Bamboo Ridge*. The poems were composed through 2008; one gets a sense of seasonal and social change as well as the whole quotidian gamut of life and, also, through the device of beginning the following poem with the last line of the previous one, a sense of multiple consciences and perspectives through these four gifted and vital poets. I wholeheartedly recommend this emotionally intelligent book that teaches us to be attentively human and to celebrate or heal memories great and intimate.

—**Robert Sullivan**, author of *Star Waka* and *Voice Carried My Family*

From King Kamehameha to Barack Obama, *Webster's Dictionary* to the *'opiuma* tree, from koi to white ginger, from ropes made of women's braids to chili pepper water—these four poets from Hawai'i prove there is no subject that *renshi*, a Japanese form of linked poetry, cannot contain. As the poems are passed collaboratively to one another, each poet ruminates on the lifelines they are struggling with and celebrating with the distinctive voice of a distinguished string quartet. A joy to read, this book would be a treasure to teach.

—**Nell Altizer**, Professor Emerita of English and Creative Writing
University of Hawai'i – Mānoa

No Choice but to Follow

TABLE OF CONTENTS

Introduction 13

The Poems

January

How Does Bamboo Ridge – Jean Yamasaki Toyama 23

Plug Along – Juliet S. Kono 24

The Next Life – Ann Inoshita 25

Into the Wild – Christy Passion 26

February

No Choice but to Follow – Jean Yamasaki Toyama 27

He Just Had to Make Sure – Juliet S. Kono 28

What Will Become of Them? – Ann Inoshita 29

Breathe; a seduction – Christy Passion 30

March

Jalousied Window – Jean Yamasaki Toyama 31

Coming Home – Juliet S. Kono 32

Embrace – Ann Inoshita 33

One Page – Christy Passion 34

April

Faithless, without Memory – Jean Yamasaki Toyama 35

Of Our Remembrances – Juliet S. Kono 37

My Memory of Your Eyes – Ann Inoshita 39

Smile in the Wind – Christy Passion 40

May

He Feels His Tumor Grow – Jean Yamasaki Toyama 42

All That Unknowing – Juliet S. Kono 43

Shattered Water – Ann Inoshita 45

Hear the Dogs Crying – Christy Passion 46

June

Do You Know My Name? – Jean Yamasaki Toyama 48

Face Looking from the Mirror – Juliet S. Kono 49

Before She Leaves – Ann Inoshita 50

From the Clouds – Christy Passion 51

July

From this Darkness – Jean Yamasaki Toyama 53

Buzzing Along with Us – Juliet S. Kono 54

Without Meaning to Be Cruel – Ann Inoshita 56

She Asked – Christy Passion 58

August

All We Do Not Know – Jean Yamasaki Toyama 59

Of the Whys and Wherefores – Juliet S. Kono 60

We're Here – Ann Inoshita 62

It Was Morning – Christy Passion 63

September

Canvas – Jean Yamasaki Toyama 65

It Was Like Finding Gold – Juliet S. Kono 66

The Uncreated – Ann Inoshita 67

The Room Fills with – Christy Passion 68

October

Trying to Warn Me – Jean Yamasaki Toyama 69

There'll Be Hell to Pay – Juliet S. Kono 70

To Have or Need – Ann Inoshita 71

Depending on Lights to Guide My Way – Christy Passion 72

November

The Fires – Jean Yamasaki Toyama 73

Let the Great Healing Begin – Juliet S. Kono 74

Shine of Tears – Ann Inoshita 75

Prepare to Move into the White House – Christy Passion 76

December

Just Enough Shave Ice – Jean Yamasaki Toyama 77

Not Pau Yet – Juliet S. Kono 78

What Had Been – Ann Inoshita 79

Fade – Christy Passion 80

Commentary 83

On Linked Poetry – Jean Yamasaki Toyama 141

About the Poets 149

CD Playlist 151

No Choice but to Follow:
Introduction

What happens when four women poets devote a year to writing poems that are inspired by a single line and do it in public on the web? This book follows our journey through a year of writing *renshi*, linked poetry. The rules were simple: each poet, in turn, would write a poem using the last line of the previous poet's poem as the basis for her own title or first line. The poem had to be posted by Sunday midnight on the Bamboo Ridge Press website and the next poet would have a week to write. By the end of the year, we had created 48 new poems and, although we really didn't know each other and wrote in very different styles and voices, our poetry and our lives were connected. Sound easy? We had *No Choice but to Follow.*

◈

In 1991 Joseph Stanton, Wing Tek Lum, and I created a book of *renshi* under the leadership of Makoto Ooka, an eminent poet from Japan. Ooka had been touring the world to promote collaborative poetry writing. It was part of a program on multilingual poetry for the University of Hawai'i Summer Session that year. The volume, *What the Kite Thinks* (University of Hawai'i Press, 1994), was the result of our writing together. In his introduction Ooka wrote, "this volume of linked verse from Hawai'i seems to me perhaps the richest in content, and the most likely to provide the reader with a sense of just what linked poetry is and what possibilities experimentation with it might reveal."

A few years later, in 1996, I convinced Eleanor Wilner and Nell Altizer, two distinguished poets, to write a *renshi* just for fun. We wrote for almost a year but not consistently. Partial results appeared in the *Michigan Quarterly Review* (Winter 1997). To say the least, *renshi* has been a happy experience for me.

Toward the end of 2007, Darrell Lum asked me whether I would be interested in doing a *renshi* project with a group of poets of my choosing as a commemorative activity for *Bamboo Ridge*'s 30th anniversary. To tell you the truth I didn't really know what was going to happen, how it would happen and who would participate. But writing collaboratively had been so exhilarating I wanted to explore the possibilities of the form again and agreed.

After asking several other poets and receiving a few quick "no thank yous" and "no ways," I hoped for the best. A few weeks later, with the help of writers Marie Hara and Darrell Lum, I had a team of poets: Juliet Kono, whom I knew only slightly and whose poetry I admired, and Ann Inoshita and Christy Passion, two poets I had never met nor even read but who were highly recommended.

I hoped that the chosen poets would not flake out, would not drop out, would meet every deadline; the whole process depended on the reliability of its participants. We would have one week to write our poem. This meant that when it was our turn, we would have to be a "faucet" poet—we would have to turn it on no matter what. No excuses. No one could drop out. We depended on each other. The pressure would be on. Incredibly, no one dropped out, no one missed a deadline.

The poems are printed here without much revision except for a few commas, corrected spelling, a rare word changed. It's all here, beauty marks and all. The real thing.

In May 2008, at the Hawai'i Book and Music Festival, all four poets got together in person for the first time. We read what we had done to date, January through April, on stage in the Mission Memorial Auditorium. It was our first time reading together and, according to editors Eric Chock and Darrell Lum, a magical moment. We had not thought about publication or recording our voices but the idea of a book and CD began. We had another opportunity to read together for *Aloha Shorts*, Hawaii Public Radio's local literature program, in September and learned how our voices worked together, each one distinct yet linked through the shared lines.

For the book, we asked each poet to recall the challenge of creating her poem each month. The month-by-month commentary follows the poems and gives insight into each person's writing process. We have also included an essay on *renshi* and linked poetry for those who wish to learn more about the poetic form and how our poems fit into this tradition. Finally, we asked each poet to contribute to the introduction by summarizing her experience. The comments appear in reverse order, so at last, Christy gets to go first!

Jean Yamasaki Toyama
Project coordinator

☙

Christy Passion:

By summarize, do you mean opening your soul and exposing the underbelly of the process such as:

— the initial compelling need to make it perfect giving way in the third month to the compelling need to turn in anything on time,

— being star struck about working with JULIET S. KONO, while pressuring out more because you are working with JULIET S. KONO, causing one to originally submit work that was already worked on, instead of completely from the ground up, because at least you could trust that, and you wouldn't be the junkest poet in the group—posting it—Yippee!—then realizing the process was cheated—boo—then feeling that originality mattered more, so having to revise a poem from the last line up, which resulted in an okay poem but felt pretty clever in the process,

— how I now hate the word "wind" and any subject that has an "airy" quality to it,

— that deadlines actually produce results,

— that I was sad when my fellow poets never told me my poems were good after posting them (we didn't talk at all, incommunicado),

— that I wanted to write to each of them after I saw their work submitted and congratulate them but didn't want to seem like a dork,

— that I was happy for a week when Jean e-mailed (first time!) me that she liked my Obama poem,

— that if you have doubts about your work, you cannot fester too long, because before you know it, another poem is due,

— that I was flabbergasted when JULIET S. KONO told me she liked my poems at the taping (her husband too),

— that I felt a sense of community when Ann told me I should apply for my English degree and we both were so excited about being published, even though we were alternate choices for this *renshi* gig (ha ha, too bad for you guys who neva like do um, eye of the tiger, baby),

— that if I knew this was going to be published from the get-go, I would not have learned how to let poems come through me naturally, it would have choked the life out of most of them, and that I would have liked for the process to continue cuz it's a good process.

You mean stuff like that?

Ann Inoshita:

When I agreed to be a part of this *renshi* project, I was grateful to work with talented authors, but I was extremely nervous that I would have writer's block. After all, what is the likelihood that I *wouldn't* have writer's block during the entire year?

It is an honor to follow a Juliet S. Kono poem because her lines are beautiful. Since I had no control over what Juliet's last line would be, I wrote poems about topics that I usually don't write about, which in hindsight is something that I recommend everyone do.

After posting my poem on the Bamboo Ridge website, I wondered if others liked my poem. Regarding the *renshi*, I experienced a lot of self-doubt and stress throughout the year. I kept reminding myself that this project is a good exercise for creativity whenever I felt strained. When I reread my poems, there were some poems that I wished I had more time to work on. Although we were linked together via the *renshi* poems, we usually didn't discuss the poems with each other during the creation process. It was a relief to know that Jean, Juliet, and Christy felt the same emotions

I felt, when we all met at the Hawaiʻi Book and Music Festival and read our poems.

Overall, I'm glad that I said "yes" to the *renshi* project, and I enjoyed the shared experience with poets Jean, Juliet, and Christy. I hope everyone who has been on this journey with us continues on their own writing journey.

Juliet S. Kono:

Difficultly. This is how I went through the year. Because everyone blew me away as each poem was posted, I hit the wall each time I had to continue the *renshi*. And talk about being envious: I wanted the straight-to-the-point lines of Jean's poems, the groundedness of Ann's poems, the amazing images of Christy's poems. I had many "now, why couldn't you write like that?" moments after reading these women's poems. If there had to be something redeeming, I suppose it had to be the summer months, during which time I actually enjoyed writing the poems. For the rest of the time, school was an interference, and I suggest that others who wish to undertake a project such as this give each person *at least* two weeks to write.

Agonizingly. After the first few poems, everything else felt like disaster. Writing the rest of the poems was like flying by the seat of my pants. An admission: I winged it most of the time. It was also like being in college all over again—under the same kind of pressures to write something, *anything*—doing the overnighters and drinking the requisite gallons of coffee (more like tea) when good sleep and a nice glass of wine were preferable. With the appearance of Jean's last line, I usually had to think about it for a couple of days then begin my writing, writing, and more writing. The short time to create the poem, the unnaturalness of having to use someone's last line, the artificiality of the whole project, made for many hand-wringing occasions with the occasional "Ugh!" and "Why did I say that I was going to do this?"

Gratefully. (Looking at the project in another way.) I accepted each last line. I also accepted each comma, period, semi-colon, word, line, poem, as blessings—of gold coins, beams of light, the diamond mind. I marveled at the scope, I rejoiced at all that was produced, I marveled at the breadth and depth of what was generated in the allotted time. I found how truly wonderful the mind is and can be under pressure. I acknowledge and accept the times when the mind didn't want to give anything, too. In addition, I was surprised by the themes of perseverance, death, life, politics, that evolved and revolved as we sang.

Sincerely. I extend my deepest appreciation to my fellow writers. What a group, and, yah, we did it! My thanks to Jean and Ann for the straightforwardness in their writing—the clarity—and to Christy for showing me her fresh, unique images. (Something for me to work toward; I learned that when you get old, you get stale.) My thanks for the unusual one-year journey that in retrospect I gained a lot in undertaking, and lastly, my very special thanks to Jean for all the work in putting this together.

Jean Yamasaki Toyama:

I've had to practice denial through my years of struggle with writer's block. I deny that I care about how good the writing is; I deny that I care what other people think about it; I deny that I want to be praised for my words. Even when I feel sad that no one has commented on anything, I push that feeling out of my mind. (And no one said anything to me about my poems for months. Not a word.)

Doubts? Plenty of them. Hesitation? All the time. I would sit at my desk trying to decide to press the insert button at the BR website. But usually after a week, my denial button would work, and I wouldn't think about my poem. I would have three weeks of freedom.

Around Friday I would check out the site to see if Juliet had posted her poem; it usually happened on Sunday, but sometimes it was earlier. Then, Ann. The suspense was greatest with Christy's poems. That was the hand-off. Would I drop it? Or run with it?

Being forced to follow, being forced to write a poem a month, having no choice for a beginning was good for me. I couldn't think about writer's block. But the personal importance of the project wasn't made clear to me until the summer of 2008 when we had a reading at the Book and Music Festival. That's when I met Ann and Christy for the first time.

Without rehearsal—stone cold—we read. We moved on cue according to our turn. Our voice was strong. I experienced a nice high. So did everyone else.

This event convinced the powers that be that our *renshi* should be published. This again imposed a discipline to my undisciplined writing. I need obligations to write, not choices. Thank you, Bamboo Ridge.

No Choice but to Follow:
The Poems

JANUARY

How Does Bamboo Ridge?

With lots of hands, lots of head, lots of heart
And hours and days, and years—30—of time.

What did bamboo ridge?
Ninety-one issues,
Eight hundred-fifty plus writers and artists
of poems, stories, plays, and essays
with plenty, plenty of words, some pictures,
some photos
To launch careers
To help pass the time
To keep hope alive

Hang on, keep watch,
Plug along.

—Jean Yamasaki Toyama

Plug Along

That's the way we do it.
In the early mornings,
far into the night,
on planes, in cafes,
or during a work break.
We turn the words over
in our heads while walking
or driving to the supermarket
or taking the children to school;
turn our worlds over
to churn out the stories,
cast our nets wide,
to pull in the memories
of our heartaches,
the sorrow of our dreams,
the lost child, the collapsed lung,
the broken wing.
The fear of them.
There we meet the flowers
that bordered the house,
cans we kicked,
bicycles we rode,
knees we scraped.
We greet our families,
our mothers and fathers,
and the other-dead.
Always the dead
whose bones toll the coming
of the next life and line.

—Juliet S. Kono

The Next Life

She heard prayers
and saw her husband
make sandwiches,
drive to work,
and pay bills.

She watched her child
write alphabet letters,
pick up stones on the sidewalk,
and run in their yard.

She looks out
waiting for arrivals—
a husband, a daughter.
All returning
discussing delights
and risks
after years of separation.

Here is a resting point
where spirits gather
until all go back
and are released
into the wild.

—Ann Inoshita

Into the Wild

I know all your stories Maori dancer
they are mine too. How you
were born of the sky but carry fire,
the waka you ride with brother whale just below

I know what you hunt,
how bristles on the skin are boiled off
the soft flesh that will be enjoyed tonight

I also know your animal eye
wants the marking of this woman,
a distant child of Kahiki too.

Beyond my pale skin far past these
brown eyes, into the wild, you can hear it

my mother's blood coursing through
my heart's chambers pulsing
moʻo women, maile leaves, flashes
of dark teeth more savage than you or I

You ask, "Do you know the dance?"

Not in Maori, my love, but in Hawaiian—
kawelu, lele, kuʻi, and feet turn
on the pounding of an ipuheke.
My feet have always known,
they are closest to our ancestors.
My body has no choice but to follow

—Christy Passion

FEBRUARY

No Choice but to Follow

Certainly she was
behind him,
he thought, as he ascended the narrow
ledge out of the unforgiving shadow.

Naturally, spring follows winter,
the full moon, the dark.
No doubt she was there.
Yet, he stopped,
looked back.

He just had to make sure.

—Jean Yamasaki Toyama

He Just Had to Make Sure

I did too.
I ran back to the house.

I saw that nothing had changed.
The fish, swimming
in loose circles
under the same stars
nesting in the trees.

Rooms, cupping
our laughter
poured into the hands
of the mornings.

Our pillow whispers,
roaming,
lazy as sleep walkers.

Our eyes, holding fast
to the white flowers
in the window-ledge light.
Still.

But I did notice that the sunline across
the porch was different,
its shadow having deepened.

Oh love, in a few years,
what will become of us?

—Juliet S. Kono

What Will Become of Them?

A woman caught
the girl's smile
when she held gardenia
for the first time.

At two o'clock,
the wind exhaled
as summer cooled
under the mango tree.

What will become of them—
a mother, a daughter.
Time seeping through their skins
until they are pulled back
to the starting place
where they wondered
what it feels like
to breathe.

—Ann Inoshita

Breathe; a seduction

Before the locked door,
the starched white sheets,
the Freud-speak,
there was a way in.
An unguarded door—
the eyes the lips
grab the handle;
skin raw sugar
turn the key;
my neck wet grass.
You say I love you with
an old rising force that
carries your breath like
orange orchids streaming down
a long stemmed waterfall
ferrying to the edge,
and my heart beats and my heart beats
salt brimmed electric novas
Breathe.
I am ruined, you are resurrected
I am the lion, and you the lamb.
The missing button and buckle
of these loose ends,
as permanent as sliced moonlight
through my jalousied window

—Christy Passion

MARCH

Jalousied Window

I see her look at you:
she tilts her head ever so cutely
and laughs so brightly.

I close the slats
against that look
hers
and yours, those half opened eyes taking in all
that light from her white teeth.

I close it shut, then open,
she's gone and you walk up the steps,
coming home.

—Jean Yamasaki Toyama

Coming Home

You were once told,
"No matter what happens
you can always
come home."

Come home,
I'll be waiting.
So will the fields,
the tree by your window,
the collection
of Matchbox cars on the sill.

Your room is as you left it.
Clothes that smell of you
remain in the closet.

I haven't had the heart to . . .

Should you walk up the hill,
I will see from my kitchen window,
the flurry of the roadside grass
in the rising dust.
I will drop the potato I'm peeling,
and my hands will fly to my mouth.
I will run out to greet you.

Embrace as you breeze by.

—Juliet S. Kono

Embrace

Voices from book pages
let me forget the daily noise
so I embrace words
as the pages exhale.

Time does not matter
when I relate
to aches and delights.

Somehow everything
is bearable
one page at a time.

—Ann Inoshita

One Page

Pressed between Webster's *gotten* and *grand*,
mama keeps your letter, one page,
to remind me when I'm at a loss for words.

Those words always the same;
I'm sorry mama, I understand now, soon real soon
but your release got pushed back twice since
then, already seven years ago. I see

your dashed out script, the curves
of *d*'s and *b*'s never touching the base—detached;
your subconscious slip, my missed warning sign like
the forged checks, threats to mama at her work,
or finding Jesus four more times before
the cops finally took you away.

It was hard on her the first few years,
hard being patted down for visits, smiling while
ignoring each new tat, but I had to settle
with the bank, play deaf to whispering neighbors
at the Safeway, at the Chevron, at the . . .

Who goin' hire him when he get out?
I cup mama's weathered hands in mine, wounded birds trembling
God goin' take care, God goin' take care

Finding the right words I need
I move you in between *irresponsible*
and *irretrievable*. Close this book,
faithless, without memory

—Christy Passion

APRIL

Faithless, without Memory

He didn't think about the after
or the before for that matter,
the time it didn't work,
the time all failed
the time we said, no, no, no,
never again.

No, he didn't think about that.

He just meddled and muddled
believing it would work
without plan
without knowledge
without loss
of our sons, our daughters,
our husbands, our wives,
our fathers, our mothers
our friends and acquaintances
names in the newspapers
names on the newscasts,
all 4273 of them
with more to come,

believing it could be done
without caring about the nameless
other sons and daughters, wives and husbands,
fathers and mothers, friends and acquaintances
whose names will not appear

with all the other
names to be written
on the marble waves

crushing the shores
of our remembrance.

—Jean Yamasaki Toyama

Of Our Remembrances

We don't want to remember
what illuminates
the smallness of our hearts,
as on the morning
I saw you grip your knees
and break into a cold perspiration
that glistened on your face
like glycerin tears.

I wanted to be off,
out of the house,
and free of you—
the gnarly trees
of your age and fears,
of what you called
your "naughty" illness
that hindered my
run across the meadows.

Tucking the nitro tablet
under the log of your tongue,
I patted your hand
and released you
to your knot of pain.
I didn't wait to see—
was the pill working?

I had make-up to apply,
last minute notes to make,
the laundry to take out.
You called to me,
asked if I would massage

the pain in your back and arm.
"I don't have time," I said,
your howling eyes
following me out the door.

It was not the usual angina.
A flaw had sent you toppling.
Until today,
I can't look into
my memory of your eyes.

—Juliet S. Kono

My Memory of Your Eyes

In album pages, I look
at thirty-year-old photos—
a skinny girl with short black hair
parted to the side
with a pin
securely placed
by her mother.

Her eyes hold
personality,
joy,
and unknowing.

I place my finger
on a photo
holding the girl's hand
glad that the camera
saved her eyes
when time
did not spin
and take everything.

These are the eyes of a girl
who is outside
smiling in the wind.

—Ann Inoshita

Smile in the Wind

Many years later,
he watches her sleep
the white hair, hollow skin, frozen
lines dwindling. He can't remember her laugh—

down at the boathouse by the Ala Wai
where dances were held every Saturday night.
So many parked cars they had to walk as far
as three blocks, but they could hear it
from that distance, the bass, the horns
taste the Latin notes as they held hands under
a copper sky hurrying toward the lighted pavilion.
Arthur Lyman's band wailing as they stepped
over conga beats towards the boys from McKinley
wearing pomade ducktails and tailored shirts.
Acknowledges them with a smirk, one arm around her
and the other raised high, a king over his court.
A good time, a lifetime, but there were also

accusations over lunch breaks, *How come you no answer
da phone when I call?* Every smile a threat
*Why he looking at you—you fucken whore.
Stay home, shit—* but baby needs
diapers and the electric is two months late
A difficult time, a lifetime, cutting him at all sides

*No good Filipino boy—yeah da truck driva
fo Love's Bakery—get dat nice-looking hapa girl,
What she doing wit him? Too bad yeah.*
Rusty nails through his shoe

He goes out to the rainy porch now, lights another
Marlboro. Glimpses her smile in the smoke
curling back in the wind. Takes another drag,
feels his tumor grow.

—Christy Passion

MAY

He Feels His Tumor Grow

That's what he calls it, that thing inside him
he doesn't know what.
Surely, the naming will tame it:
tumor, tumor. Then, it will
stop growing,
this feeling.
In him, on him, by him, with him . . .
he uses prepositions to make him think he knows.
He doesn't.
When did it start? It was always there,
never there.

He says his but doesn't know why.
He doesn't possess it,
even know it,
but there it is,
his;
he feels it
somewhere
growing:

all that unknowing.

—Jean Yamasaki Toyama

All That Unknowing

of what lay beneath the glassy surface
of the sea before you,
made you want to dive,
deep,
into its dark-blue secrets
and trapped air.

You have finally reached bottom.
Now, you are heading up,
as if in an unwinding
of your life's journey.
So your dying
comes as no surprise,
except to those who thought you'd live
forever. They deceptively cling to you,
as they would a life raft,
and in the end, to life itself.

You need this time
to grieve for yourself,
times you fetched
the morning paper from the stoop,
turned over the frying rice,
or helped your daughter with her sweater.
All life's work.
But to them this grieving means
that you are giving up the sky
or that burst of moonlight above you.
They make you feel guilty
for having lost your hat to the wind,
for not trying harder to beat your illness.

But I see it in your eyes.
You are holding onto nothing.
You are finding
that there's a certain
grace and relief
in acknowledging
your fatalistic move up
toward the light-flushed surface,
as when you first dove in,
at birth,
and shattered the water.

—Juliet S. Kono

Shattered Water

She ran past the weathered houses,
fenced gardens, and crying dogs.
Air escaped from her throat,
and it was hard to breathe.
As her legs teared with sweat,
her eyes saw water running
through a canal.

She picked up a rock,
threw it at her reflection,
and shattered the water.

In the water,
pieces of herself dispersed
and reassembled.

She stared at her image.
Then, she turned around and walked
past the fenced gardens
and weathered houses.

She could still hear the dogs crying.

—Ann Inoshita

Hear the Dogs Crying

A recording of her voice, an old woman's voice
full of gravel and lead steeped through
the car radio. She spoke of gathering limu
visitors on ships, and dusty roads in Waiʻanae.
In the distance you could almost hear
the dogs crying, the mullet wriggling in the fish bag

Nostalgic for a tutu I never knew,
I feel the ocean pulse inside me
waves rolling over, pushing me till I leap
from this car through the congested H-1
across the noise and ashen sky

emerge beneath the rains in Nuʻuanu.
I move past the fresh water ponds
past the guava trees towards homes
with flimsy tin roofs where
my father, already late for school,
races up Papakōlea with a kite made
of fishing twine. Framed in a small kitchen
window, tutu scrapes the meat from awa skin
for dinner tonight, wipes her hands on
old flour bags for dish cloths.
She is already small and wants to forget
I may be too late—

I have tomatoes and onion from the market, tutu,
my hand is out, my plate is empty
and some bones for the dogs to stop their crying
do you know my name?

I am listening for your stories to call me in
my hand is out, my plate is empty
for your stories to show me the way
tutu, do you know my name?

—Christy Passion

JUNE

Do You Know My Name?

It just irked her no end when she couldn't pull out the name
that should have matched the face in front of her.

She had in the past been able to grab a sliver of a syllable,
a letter like an "M" that led to Martha or Milly or
some clue that pulled out a name.
When no letter came, she'd look at the face
and went through the alphabet: a, b, c, d, e . . .
until some sound from inside came out through
her tongue: Emma?
No, not Emma.
She waited for that feeling of relief, a confirmation
that she could remember.

So, do you know my name? asked
the face looking from the mirror.

—Jean Yamasaki Toyama

The Face Looking from the Mirror

Isn't rounder
or stronger.
Not a face to be afraid
of in its song.
It is kinder,
more gentle,
glow-softened
by petticoat-white
lights, ruffled
as oncidium orchids.

. . . stares out in longing
for a simple kiss,
the precision of nesting tables,
the pin-wheel whites,
along the walkway
that brushed her skirts
as she walked by
and passed through sorrow,
of her life
and you.
The sky in the mirror
is blue, the grass green
and you want
to bring her flowers,
write her a poem
before she leaves.

—Juliet S. Kono

Before She Leaves

Blue flowers open
near the cement pathway
and she walks down
porch steps.

The sky is lovely
as she breathes in
and walks to the car.

She has books to read
and lesson plans to prepare
for her first classes in the fall.

Before she leaves,
she looks up
to see birds flying
from the clouds.

—Ann Inoshita

From the Clouds

Father Sky looked down
on all the beauty of Mother Earth
the hills, the valleys, then clasped her tightly.
So close was the embrace, their children;
the winds, the forests, the birds
only knew darkness

On their knees and shoulders, the children
pushed them, no—ripped them apart so they
could live in the light. Father Sky grieved much.

Grandma grieves much.
Another week of that breathing tube
for you Grandpa, another week of bloody
brown urine, beeping monitors and repentant nurses
"I'm so sorry, so sorry."

We go to the chapel to pray, on our knees
she to the god of medicine, and I—
I dig my knees deep into this church pew, dig beneath
the dirty shag rug through the floor boards till
my knees rip the stitches binding us here
in this endless maze of tubes and feeble doctors.
On my shoulders I hold back Grandma's tears
your wedding vows and first home in Pālolo valley.
The small things so heavy now, I carry too;
your calloused hands,
the smell of sardines and chili pepper water,
mending old fishing nets in the early morning.

I pray to cut the anchor of your sinking vessel
I pray you catch the tail of the wind

I pray a small light to lead you from this darkness

—Christy Passion

JULY

From this Darkness

I see a small light
green and glowing.
It moves from side to side
like the sagelampu I carried
for you, Mama.
You said,
"Quick get the lamp, Tanouesan has a high fever."
I held the lamp in front of us and the light
would zigzag along the dirt path
in rhythm with our footfalls.
Your healing cups would clink in time
with the crunch of dirt and small stones under our feet.
We were alone except for frogs croaking in the dark
and the iridescent
bugs
buzzing along with us.

—Jean Yamasaki Toyama

Buzzing Along with Us

are your companions in life—
your memories—
that can spring out of nowhere.
Take you to a childhood afternoon
or light a mountain trail
you once walked—
the same light attenuated by bamboo,
swaying in the wind's coming—
where a fall off the precipice
meant no returning
to the porch shaded
by the jacaranda.
Or, a sudden face
you had not thought of in years
may flash before you,
young as you saw it last,
but wouldn't recognize, today.
They take your hands,
never let them go.
They make no neat patterns in your mind.
They may play tricks
or impress upon you,
a longing,
for the times she wore
the water-lily dress
that floated around her in a cloud,
cupped the white ginger in her hands,
or dreamed of banquets
when she no longer could eat.
Even that, once more.
Warm or chilling,
they stay with you

like a quiet child might,
or a noisy one,
but always at your side without apology,
waiting to take you down
the street you ran on
with your sad old dog
or the wobbly bicycle wheel
you rolled with a stick
in the spindle of summer
that unraveled the threads of your life.
They bring up matters
that send sentimental tears
down your cheeks;
feed into your old heartaches.
And oftentimes, in your recollections,
you pass them off
to your children
without ever meaning to be cruel.

—Juliet S. Kono

Without Meaning to Be Cruel

One teacha asked me if I wanted fo be his teacha's aide fo Biology class.
My classmates said was good fo be one teacha's aide
cuz you just help and das it.
Not like you one student in class and gotta do class work.
Was my senior year and I had most of da credits fo graduate
so I decided fo be his teacha's aide.

I ran errands fo him and did stuffs like enter grades into his grade book.
Layda on, he told me dat dea was going be one teacha fo replace him
cuz he got one nodda job.

Da new teacha was one lady who look like she just graduated college.
One day, she brought one glass tank wit white mice inside.
She had to leave fo get someting, and I was in charge of da class.
Everybody was studying, so I looked inside da tank.
I saw one mouse go by da odda mouse.
Look like da mouse was pulling off da odda mouse's hairs.
I dunno if dis normal. I wanted da pulling fo stop,
so I started poking da mouse wit one stick.
Da mouse neva stop, so I kept poking um.

Everybody gathered around da tank.
Layda, da mouse finally stopped pulling.
I was still holding da stick.
I shoulda told everybody fo go back to dea desks, but I neva.
I wanted fo make sure da mouse neva pick on da odda mouse again.
I kept poking.
Da mouse's head started fo twitch.

Wen da teacha came back, everybody went back to dea desks.
She asked da class wat happened.
Everybody looked at me and neva say nothing.

She started da lesson as I looked inside da tank.
Why da mouse gotta keep twitching laidat?
I hoped da mouse would stop twitching next class
but it neva.

Every class, I look da tank and wish I neva do wat I did.
Da teacha saw da mouse, and I no can look her in da eye
wen she asked me wat happened.

—Ann Inoshita

She Asked

What to give you?

The black bird or the perfect arc
it made while flying upward over

green cypress reminding me of
Roman coliseums and grander things

than this three story walk-up.
Perhaps a moment, which expanded

and breathed when I saw
fragile translucent star blossoms

a field of them blanketing the lawn
that one day will be our home.

And I wasn't afraid.
A song, I'll give you a song

to sing to the rocks we will use
to fill that defunct septic tank.

They'll carry that tune to the
wooden beams of our future,

hammered together by hands that pray
with gratitude for all we do not know.

—Christy Passion

AUGUST

All We Do Not Know

That remains a mystery to me:

the nature of dark matter—MACHOs or Massive Compact Halo
Objects, WIMPs or Weakly Interacting Massive Particles and neutrinos,
those billion to one particles
for every proton and electron in the universe,

the nature of dark energy—cosmological constant, scalar fields
energizing the accelerating expansion of the universe

the reality of hyperspace in ten dimensions making possible time
travel on the warping and rippling of space

the promise of superstrings which will unite stars and galaxies with
the molecules
of my own DNA

makes me hungry

for the big and small of it,
for the fast and slow of it
for the hot and cold of it;
for the ins and outs

of the whys and wherefores.

—Jean Yamasaki Toyama

Of the Whys and Wherefores

we ponder.
Pull them out,
as from a magician's hat.

Small at first,
the questions—
like the easy trick
of making a quarter appear
from the petal of a child's ear
that makes him smile and run
to his mother and say, "Look what I've got!"
Of spouting a lifeline of blood-red scarves
from hands that we can swear were empty
the last time we looked,
the answers more cloudy.

How are we going to pull this off,
produce a dove from a sleeve
a hand or head,
another then another—a small flock?
An illusionist will tell you
that handling what is real
takes more care.

But in the end, it's the disappearing
acts that hold our attention.
The mystery of it all.
We want to know why
we can't see the wind
or where meteor showers
come from, where they go,
giving us the perfect

opportunity to ask—
why we're here, then not.

—Juliet S. Kono

We're Here

We return to the pond
where a koi slaps the water
and a turtle dives in.
As water falls into the pond,
I hear you breathe.

A dragonfly passes
and a sparrow hops
through the weeds.
As we sit in the shade,
I hear you breathe.

You will leave soon
and summer is ending.
As I hold you tight,
I hear you breathe.

The sky dims
and the wind is cool.
As we walk to the car,
I hold my breath
wishing it was morning.

—Ann Inoshita

It Was Morning
(on viewing Choris's portrait of Kamehameha I)

It was morning when I first saw you
on a slim side wall where
someone might absentmindedly flip
a light switch. Not the center of the gallery
with guards flanking you, cordoned off
by velvet ropes. Instead

you are housed in a small common frame
constricted by a fading red vest.
Your gray hair creates a halo effect;
a pious merchant, an aging choirboy. Impostor.

Where are you, my king?

You are there, a shadow on the horizon
amidst a fleet of ten, a hundred, a thousand,
engulfing as the waves that surround this island,
seated on the ama, eyes perched on the shores of Waikīkī.
You are there in the tall grass of Nuʻuanu,
sun gleaming off your thighs, your chest.
Moʻo skin helmets your face allowing
only the black pupil widening to be seen,
your calloused hand holding back the spear
anxious for the release. You are there
in the first clashes of muscle and teeth,
salt sweat drawing light onto your skin
as the ʻelepaio shrieks in the branches above.
Your spear tip pushes father and brother to the edge
Imua! Imua! and 400 more leap like mullets
into stony nets waiting below.

A pact of silence has been made by the bones left behind,
I go to those pastures to break it. I go to listen
to find you, my king. Too many have been misled by this canvas.

—Christy Passion

SEPTEMBER

Canvas

An old canvas bag tucked in between tattered boxes
lying on the floor of the storage room crisscrossed
by cobwebs:
I'm selling the family house.

The canvas is yellow, splotched with brown hues
covered with dust from the ages.
Whose canvas bag?
I untie the knot that holds the heavy contents:
standard sized hammer, medium chisel, a few
five-inch nails.

The rough surface of the canvas, the smell of lost time
scrape away the years and I see my father
coming home from work
tired, but happy to see us, his daughters.
We climb over him and empty his pant cuffs.
The sawdust of the day spills out.

It's like finding gold.

—Jean Yamasaki Toyama

It Was Like Finding Gold

After the fire,
an act of devotion.
Thousands of women cut
their hair for the thigh-thick braids
of hair ropes that lifted
the heavy spruce beams
taken from medieval loam.
Ordinary ropes would not have been able
to lift and have these beams loom over
worshippers in the Grand Amida Hall
after the rebuilding of the Eastern Temple.

Of high gloss—
ebony but gold, more—
the hair ropes lifted the burden
of the women's attachment.
As I looked into the glass
display case of their sacrifice,
I touched my own hair
and thought of hair
that lifted the beams
up toward the open rafters,
up toward the stars
and up toward the moon.
Upward and outward
toward nothing
and the uncreated.

—Juliet S. Kono

The Uncreated

She lies on her bed and stares at the ceiling
while her body is heavy from a cold.

The smell of miso soup and warm squash
cooked in dashi, shoyu, and sugar
comes from the kitchen.

As she looks at her empty notepad,
she sees the clock's rotating hand.

She stares at the uncreated
until words assemble and sounds connect.
The room fills with stories.

—Ann Inoshita

The Room Fills with

images like a Frida Kahlo painting;
a woman falling from a New York city skyscraper
bloodied with eyes wide open, images
of brutality in a Dominican Republic cane field
against large breasted young girls shining
in their last breath, all of it for love, love, love.
Images of you and I at the cafe where I learned to like coffee
pouring over frivolous details to you and you
learned women were much better weak better
than they could ever be strong in all their tender parts.
See the flutter of her dress
see the dust rising from the field
see me look up with butterfly lids
pregnant with tears folded over like proteas, descending
from such heights into the *shsk shsk*
of Waimanalo brush and the wild eyes of a mongoose staring
out at us that night when the moon was full and our hearts were full
with the yellow eyes of a lion
trying to warn me.

—Christy Passion

OCTOBER

Trying to Warn Me

They warned them about us, about me.
We were one of them.
Not to be trusted, they said.

Don't talk so loud, she said.
Speak English, she said.
So I went to my room and hid my dolls with wobbly heads.

They'll be coming, don't you doubt it, they'll be coming
and we'll be blamed
because of the curve of our nose,
the slant of our eyes.
Mark my words,
there'll be hell to pay.

—Jean Yamasaki Toyama

There'll Be Hell to Pay

And we are paying,
the Dow falling
precipitously in the shale of greed.

Now I have portion control.
My husband grows thinner.
I divvy up the stone potatoes, stone carrots.
I go around to turn off unnecessary lights.
We eat in, take home-lunch to work,
five minute showers, search for black
currents and unplug computers.
We eat no fat and dream lean.
Teeth against the meat bone.
We do whatever it takes,
as we watch the rock of our pensions
disappear over the cliff.
Where did it all go?
"To money heaven," you say.
"Just to money heaven."

I go outside to look
up at the sky.
I see that it is all there—
the pebbles of clouds,
the ambient crystals of light,
a blue-rock sky
that's not bad
to have or need.

—Juliet S. Kono

To Have or Need

My battery alarm clock buzzed at 4:30 a.m.,
and I walked toward my parents' voices
as the radio talked about the power outage
and we listened with flashlights.

I brushed my teeth, put on makeup,
and changed clothes in dim light.
Then I carried a bag containing
papers I graded the night before
grateful that there was power yesterday.

I reversed out of the driveway with caution
and measured the distance
between car headlights
as I crossed the intersection.

There were rows of lights on the freeway,
and I drove along with everyone
trying to forget the inconvenience
depending on lights to guide my way.

—Ann Inoshita

Depending on Lights to Guide My Way

Thanks to the local bradas, playing uke Friday night,
anybody's backyard, Pauoa valley. The clink
of their green bottles drifting up to moths
dancing in the porch light guiding my way.

And to Nana who comes faithfully
to early mass every Sunday,
dressed in low-heeled-square-toed shoes,
genuflecting before a mosaic of apostles
in stained glass light guiding my way.

There are others; Japanese cops in Korean bars,
Chinatown butchers chopping char siu,
the bedridden in Leahi who outlive their children.

As I set sail on this moonless life,
I go over a riverbed of stones casting off
sparks as we touch, brief lights
illuminating the long journey ahead.
I keep an eye out for the fires.

—Christy Passion

NOVEMBER

The Fires

The flames have leapt from point to point
unabated:
first our eyes
then our ears,
into our hearts
into our spleens,
our insides
scorched.

We fight each other.
Fear blinds us.

Put the fires out.
They have burned for eight years.

Let the great healing begin.

—Jean Yamasaki Toyama

Let the Great Healing Begin

He is here
to visit his dying grandmother.
She lives in an apartment
building a few blocks away
from where we live,
and where he spent his childhood,
walking to and from school
or his part-time job, scooping ice cream.

Early in the morning
while on our daily walk in the hush,
we go past the building and vow—
should we but glimpse his sorrow—
to run away
and release him to his privacy.

No one's around.
The TV vans that cover every moment
of his life sit quietly in the church
parking lot across the street.
We walk back home
and on the way,
stop beneath an 'opiuma tree
that sheds its petals in the coming light
to the shine of tears.

—Juliet S. Kono

Shine of Tears

On November 4, 2008,
a man, unlike predecessors before him,
walks to a podium in Chicago
to address a nation
with his acceptance speech.

In a shine of tears, some remember:
falling stock market
housing market
credit crisis
war.

The president-elect walks on stage
with his wife and two daughters.

There's a lot to accomplish
as Barack Obama and his family
prepare to move into the White House.

—Ann Inoshita

Prepare to Move into the White House

I imagine you would take us with you,
perhaps rolled up in a Persian rug
or tucked in hidden pockets of your luggage
carrying white shirts, socks, and underwear.

There is no need to take us out
right away, no need to show us around.
Forget about us as you do your spine or spleen.

But when old chains begin to rattle
in your mind, or on the lips of suits
lining red carpeted hallways
that no longer seem new to you

we will be there; trade winds twisting
down the Koʻolau, fragrant fallen mangos,
nests of salt. Let us offer you respite, let us
be a toe hold in the craggy wall you climb
treading a new path to a new country.

Let us remind you of when hope
was measured in pocket change
after a long day of body surfing—
just enough for shaved ice and the bus ride home.

—Christy Passion

DECEMBER

Just Enough Shave Ice

For make my lips red like strawberry
For cool me off and calm me down
afta all dis and all dat

Just enough hope for me
to think that yes we can
do this
and do that
with all we have
or don't have

Just enough time for finish my poem
For da dis of da dat

Just enough space to write
All these thirty years
We did this
We did that

And no,
We not pau yet

—Jean Yamasaki Toyama

Not Pau Yet

My father's interrogative,
"What, not pau yet? How come?"
was always followed
by my mother's declarative,
"No, not pau yet,"
followed by my unvoiced imperative,
"Do it yourself, den!"

My reflection of these moments
of a man who did nothing around the house,
is accompanied by ripples of pity
for his pools of impatience,
driven by selfishness and will
that had distorted his sense of time,
as to how long it took to iron his shirt,
cook the rice for his meals,
or fill the tub for his bath.

However much love overcomes
pity, there is an overshadowing penalty.
Love slackens in its flow,
like that of slack water,
and turns, in tidal memory,
toward indifference,
the forgetting of what had been good.

—Juliet S. Kono

What Had Been

Listen to language
centuries old
and from decades past.

Sounds were written in journals,
archived in libraries, schools, and homes.

My regards to all
who work in this endeavor
recording moments
reading memories
printing time across the page

finding ways to translate the essence
of the past
of the present
while keeping music intact
so others will learn

long after we die
and fade into the pages.

—Ann Inoshita

Fade

If I could give to you your father whole,
but I cannot give to you your father whole,
he would be free of the demons that made him
eat straight from jelly jars then
turned him into a poltergeist
shuffling through the hallways at midnight.
He would be free of the strokes, tics, and tremors
that now reside as unwelcome guests
disregarding the hour.
I would give him to you
firm and familiar like the sinewy
muscles in your arms heavy
with the wisdom gained
by a lifetime spent loving one woman,
the small triumphs,
the shifting joys.
Each memory recalled of a first—
smile, step, word, kiss would be a black strand
on his head till he stood before you
a lush young man, a reflection in the mirror
You are the common ground now, son,
you are my ladder
A blessing that one day you will give
to your own son. You would not
fear the road ahead, you would not
fear words like Alzheimer's, or cancer
or any other dark god disguised
in medical terms.
You would not shield your eyes
as he fades from view
flashing over the horizon.

—Christy Passion

No Choice but to Follow:
Commentary

JANUARY

Jean:

My biggest problem was how to start? Where to begin? That's the rub. Any artist faced with freedom flails about for a while. Yes, there would be constraints once we got started, but the constraints were really a guide to where to go. Now I had the responsibility to start.

Darrell told me I could do anything I wanted. Big help—in some ways the worst you can get. Too much freedom. So I thought about Darrell and Eric and what they had achieved in all these 30 years. It would be fitting to start with them, after all, the *renshi* was to commemorate *Bamboo Ridge*. I asked whether there was a database of all that had been published. They tell us to be careful of what we ask. I was given a ream of paper filled with hundreds of names and titles. Too much information.

I then turned to the dictionary—my place of last resort—for the meaning of "ridge": to form into a chain of hills or mountains. It got me going.

How Does Bamboo Ridge?

With lots of hands, lots of head, lots of heart
And hours and days, and years—30—of time.

What did bamboo ridge?
Ninety-one issues.
Eight hundred-fifty plus writers and artists
of poems, stories, plays, and essays
with plenty, plenty of words, some pictures, some photos
To launch careers
To help pass the time
To keep hope alive

Hang on, keep watch,
Plug along.

Juliet:

Hey, I could make the excuse that I was coerced into doing this *renshi* thing, because of Wing Tek Lum's tooth and nail, unremitting persuasion. The phone call: "C'mon Juliet, we need four poets to do this project!"—even if he did not come forward to be one of us, especially since it would have been wonderful if we had a male voice in the mix. *Teaching, school work, places to go, sermons to give, the sick to minister.* "No, no, I don't think so" had been my first reaction. But I do concede, it was probably my poet's ego that said, "yes!" Actually, it was more like "yeah, yeah, okay, okay," for it was still September or October 2007 when this project was first proposed as part of BR's 30th anniversary. I was truly unconcerned about it. It was the least of my worries. January 2008 seemed very far away, especially since my focus was on the stack of student papers on my desk.

I went through the months of November and December with no second thoughts about the project. Not much later, however, it dawned on me that I was part of this project with reminders from Darrell on how to get onto the website. With the New Year just over, I started having "Well-you-better-get-down-to-business" anxiety dreams. I got up feeling sweaty and hot. Horrified! Oh no, not hot flashes again! Out of my sleep fog, what a relief to think that it was only about writing a *few* lines of a *renshi*. From then on, I sort of hung out with my computer, while I gripped the edge of my desk and waited for that first last line.

My husband and I were traveling at the time, so I had that laptop plugged in every place we went. Whew, it finally appeared: Jean's first poem. And double whew—the last line was not *too* difficult: "Plug along." Yes, that's what she wrote "Plug along." Okay, I could write something about that—the what, where, and how we plugged on as writers. ". . . far into the night/ on planes in cafes/ during a work break . . ." I made a few drafts, wrote the poem, felt confident about the outcome, and posted it. So far so good. It was actually fun. (I must admit, that when I came to the last line of my poem, I was more worried about how I ended the poem than about Ann, the next poet who had to work with it.)

Plug Along

That's the way we do it.
In the early mornings,
far into the night,
on planes, in cafes,
or during a work break.
We turn the words over
in our heads while walking
or driving to the supermarket
or taking the children to school;
turn our worlds over
to churn out the stories,
cast our nets wide,
to pull in the memories
of our heartaches,
the sorrow of our dreams,
the lost child, the collapsed lung,
the broken wing.
The fear of them.
There we meet the flowers
that bordered the house,
cans we kicked,
bicycles we rode,
knees we scraped.
We greet our families,
our mothers and fathers,
and the other-dead.
Always the dead
whose bones toll the coming
of the next life and line.

Ann:

During the first *renshi* month, I was excited, nervous, and thankful to be in the company of talented women. Juliet was generous with her support during the publication of my first book of poems, and I looked forward to working with her. Although I had never met Jean, I knew that she had contributed poems in the book, *What the Kite Thinks*, a linked poem, with Makoto Ooka, Wing Tek Lum, and Joseph Stanton. At the University of Hawai'i at Manoa, I remember seeing Christy's name on posters as the recipient of creative writing awards. It was an honor to participate in a *renshi* with these poets, but I was concerned about creating a poem within the one-week time frame. I worked on a weekly deadline during poetry workshops in the past, but a *renshi* was different. Our poems were to be posted by the deadline on the website for everyone to see—ready or not. I was nervous and prayed that I wouldn't get writer's block for the entire year. As I saw Jean's first post, I wondered what Juliet's last line would be. I kept checking the *renshi* page on the BRP website until I saw Juliet's poem and last line "of the next life and line."

I could work with "The Next Life" as the title for my poem with a focus on the afterlife. In January I worked from a building in Honolulu with a wonderful view of the mountains, ocean, and nearby structures. This view invoked a calm, spiritual feeling. I wondered what scenario I could have regarding the afterlife, and the characters came about. The poem is about a woman who died and is watching after her husband and daughter who are still living. At the end of the poem, I wanted the characters to meet again with a happy reunion in the afterlife. When I wrote the poem, I intentionally left out information for the reader; the reader will not know that the main character is dead until the last stanza.

The Next Life

She heard prayers
and saw her husband
make sandwiches,
drive to work,
and pay bills.

She watched her child
write alphabet letters,
pick up stones on the sidewalk,
and run in their yard.

She looks out
waiting for arrivals—
a husband, a daughter.
All returning
discussing delights
and risks

after years of separation.

Here is a resting point
where spirits gather
until all go back
and are released
into the wild.

Christy:

I remember exactly the genesis of this poem. It came from looking at a picture in the *MĀNOA Journal, Varua Tupu*. It was the picture of a Polynesian male dancer in traditional costume, kneeling down, looking straight into the camera. It was a black and white photo, which enhanced the intensity of his stare, leaving any woman weak in the knees. This was also a journal in which one of my fellow *renshi* poets, Jean, had translated works. It was my first introduction to her as we would not meet face to face for many months into this project, and in my mind also solidified my place as the most novice of this grouping of poets. Both Juliet and Ann had books of poetry under their belts; Jean not only had published works but also was translating works for *MĀNOA* no less (a journal which I deeply respect). I had come along in recent times to this poetry scene, and although I have done well with awards and local publishing for my works, I felt a sense of having to prove my worth. I deliberately went with one of my differences from the other poets for this first poem, my Hawaiian ancestry.

The picture made me think of Maori men (not to mention our halau was planning to go to New Zealand in the summer so my thoughts were frequently on the Maori culture). This led me to thinking of our shared genealogy, stories, and values. For a while I had wanted to write something about the Hawaiian blood that runs through my veins, while my Portuguese skin and hair keeps this fact a secret. By taking the voice of speaking to the Maori dancer in the picture (I made him Maori whether he was or not) I could address this dichotomy in me while pulling in our lineage. The waka and the whale for the Maori, the allusion to Kamapuaʻa and sex for Hawaiians, and Kahiki, which ties our paths together. In the end, I felt especially proud of its grounding. Usually I am quite unsure of the finished poem I create. I need to tinker and get opinions before I can sleep well with it. But this one had a strength to it, an earthiness that—dare I suggest—reminded me of Lorca's discussion on *duende*. Let me be clear, I am not saying that this poem is the stuff of *duende*, although I am not saying it isn't either. It was just something that I truly felt came from the earth, up. This poem wasn't the stuff of angels, it was something a little more dangerous. I liked it.

Into the Wild

I know all your stories Maori dancer
they are mine too. How you
were born of the sky but carry fire,
the waka you ride with brother whale just below

I know what you hunt,
how bristles on the skin are boiled off
the soft flesh that will be enjoyed tonight

I also know your animal eye
wants the marking of this woman,
a distant child of Kahiki too..

Beyond my pale skin far past these
brown eyes, into the wild, you can hear it

my mother's blood coursing through
my heart's chambers pulsing
mo'o women, maile leaves, flashes
of dark teeth more savage than you or I

You ask, "Do you know the dance?"

Not in Maori, my love, but in Hawaiian—
kawelu, lele, ku'i, and feet turn
on the pounding of an ipuheke.
My feet have always known,
they are closest to our ancestors.
My body has no choice but to follow

FEBRUARY

Jean:

Christy, whom I had not met except through email, gave me "no choice but to follow." She was talking about her hula, her Maori connections. I had no choice, but I couldn't follow her dance. I scanned myself for stories about *following*. I remembered the song from *The Fantastiks*, "Follow, follow, follow," but that led nowhere.

Here is a false start, a poem I rejected:

> No choice but to follow
> He had no choice but to follow,
> the poor thing
> on a string—old, frayed,
> but securely tied.
> It hung in a half loop
> the outline of an upside down moon.
> He felt free—the string was not taut—as long
> as he followed.
> It wasn't always like that,
> before, the string stung
> in his neck, the
> runny wound still visible
> now, even without the
> string, poor Pozzo
> runs behind Lucky

Pozzo and Lucky—slave and master, master and slave—was the image I started with from Beckett's *Waiting for Godot*. I rejected the poem, too esoteric. Then I thought of Orpheus and Eurydice, Demeter and Persephone, and the Japanese woman who was supposed to follow her man ten steps behind, or so we were told. I took the male point of view, wondering who didn't have the choice.

> **No Choice but to Follow**
>
> Certainly she was
> behind him,
> he thought, as he ascended the narrow

ledge out of the unforgiving shadow.

Naturally, spring follows winter,
the full moon, the dark.
No doubt she was there.
Yet, he stopped,
looked back.

He just had to make sure.

Juliet:

February's poem worked differently. With Jean's last line, "He just had to make sure," I struggled with the "he." What was I going to do with that? Now, the pressure was on, the second week deadline coming up faster than a tidal wave. Rubbing my hands together, I said to myself—he just had to make sure, but *I did too.* These words became the genesis for the next poem. In addition, not long before this, I had been commenting to others as to how the sun line had been changing on our lanai and so had our lives and *bling!* I wanted to put the two ideas together. I brought these elements together and made the deadline. I had about three weeks to relax and enjoy the rest of the poems coming out.

He Just Had to Make Sure

I did too.
I ran back to the house.

I saw that nothing had changed.
The fish, swimming
in loose circles
under the same stars
nesting in the trees.

Rooms, cupping
our laughter
poured into the hands
of the mornings.

Our pillow whispers,
roaming,
lazy as sleep walkers.

Our eyes, holding fast
to the white flowers
in the window-ledge light.
Still.

But I did notice that the sunline across
the porch was different,
its shadow having deepened.

*Oh love, in a few years,
what will become of us?*

Ann:

In February the last line of Juliet's poem, "what will become of us," led me to think of questions many people ask themselves regarding their own future. Then, I thought of childhood and the constant wondering and concern for the future. I was still thinking spiritually from last month's poem, and I thought of the idea of spirits wondering how it is to live in a human form. I combined all of these ideas to form this poem with the title, "What Will Become of Them?"

What Will Become of Them?

A woman caught
the girl's smile
when she held gardenia
for the first time.

At two o'clock,
the wind exhaled
as summer cooled
under the mango tree.

What will become of them—
a mother, a daughter.
Time seeping through their skins
until they are pulled back
to the starting place
where they wondered
what it feels like
to breathe.

Christy:

Well this one is about sex. Again trying to take it in a different direction from the previous two poems (this month's one by Juliet was just inspiring to me), which had a feel of slow things, things winding down, a quietness. Procreation seemed the opposite. Not just sex, but the kind that binds us in, perhaps, places that we cannot fully stand firm in. I was experimenting with a different style, a stream of thought, a definite crescendo and then a softening. It did not seem right to break it into verses. I also experimented with imagery carrying the content. By the way, the image of orange orchids streaming down a long-stemmed waterfall came from looking at CT scans of kidneys.

Breathe; a seduction

Before the locked door,
the starched white sheets,
the Freud-speak,
there was a way in.
An unguarded door—
the eyes the lips
grab the handle;
skin raw sugar
turn the key;
my neck wet grass.
You say I love you with
an old rising force that
carries your breath like
orange orchids streaming down
a long stemmed waterfall
ferrying to the edge,
and my heart beats and my heart beats
salt brimmed electric novas
Breathe.
I am ruined, you are resurrected
I am the lion, and you the lamb.
The missing button and buckle
of these loose ends,
as permanent as sliced moonlight
through my jalousied window

MARCH

Jean:

Christy's "seduction" left me with "through my jalousied window" which made me think immediately of Robbe-Grillet's novel, *Jealousy*, where the husband is looking through the window at his wife and another man. In that novel so much has to do with looking. So I had a theme.

The poem came swiftly and the woman who was supposed to be watching had a voice. In my poem everyone is ogling. What I wrote in my journal was more or less the poem that follows.

> **Jalousied Window**
>
> I see her look at you:
> she tilts her head ever so cutely
> and laughs so brightly.
>
> I close the slats
> against that look
> hers
> and yours, those half opened eyes taking in all
> that light from her white teeth.
>
> I close it shut, then open,
> she's gone and you walk up the steps,
> coming home.

Juliet:

The ending line, "coming home," in March's poem seemed harmless enough. February had been my son's birthday—a time, after all these years, that does not slide into forgetfulness. I thought of how he could come home, if only as a spirit, as in wind or water. Images of living in Hilo, images of his life, my life, and how I would know him, *feel* him, if he passed me by, just passed me by, and how I would hold him became the first thoughts, then the basis, and the ending for this poem. "Embrace as you breeze by." And it was written quickly—school taking much of my time by then—and driven by the energy of grief. I did feel bad for Ann, for what could she do with a line like that—"embrace as you breeze by"? Not an easy line to do anything with. I felt apologetic.

Coming Home

You were once told,
"No matter what happens
you can always
come home."

Come home,
I'll be waiting.
So will the fields,
the tree by your window,
the collection
of Matchbox cars on the sill.

Your room is as you left it.
Clothes that smell of you
remain in the closet.

I haven't had the heart to . . .

Should you walk up the hill,
I will see from my kitchen window,
the flurry of the roadside grass
in the rising dust.
I will drop the potato I'm peeling,
and my hands will fly to my mouth.
I will run out to greet you.

Embrace as you breeze by.

Ann:

March was a challenging month for me. It was one of those months when you feel like being with family, eating a lot of home cooking, and staying under the blanket in bed a little while longer. The word "embrace" stood out from Juliet's last line. Writing has always helped me, and reading helps to focus attention away from hardships. Words are embraced and the world seems to be softer for a few hours. I hoped the last line of my poem, "one page at a time," would be enough for Christy to write a poem; I couldn't think of another way to end the poem.

Embrace

Voices from book pages
let me forget the daily noise
so I embrace words
as the pages exhale.

Time does not matter
when I relate
to aches and delights.

Somehow everything
is bearable
one page at a time.

Christy:

I had written a previous poem, "Preparing for the Prodigal Son" which was published in *Bamboo Ridge* Issue #89. It took the perspective of a brother returning from jail. "One Page" expands on this to include the voice of a parent juxtaposed against the brother who has pretty much given up hope. I am not sure what spawned "One Page," but I do know that the words *gotten* and *grand*, as well as *irresponsible* and *irretrievable* were actual word pairings I got from just allowing the dictionary to open naturally. First shots for the both of them, no poring through the dictionary to find the right combination. Lucky for me.

One Page

Pressed between Webster's *gotten* and *grand*,
mama keeps your letter, one page,
to remind me when I'm at a loss for words.

Those words always the same;
I'm sorry mama, I understand now, soon real soon
but your release got pushed back twice since
then, already seven years ago. I see

your dashed out script, the curves
of *d*'s and *b*'s never touching the base—detached;
your subconscious slip, my missed warning sign like
the forged checks, threats to mama at her work,
or finding Jesus four more times before
the cops finally took you away.

It was hard on her the first few years,
hard being patted down for visits, smiling while
ignoring each new tat, but I had to settle
with the bank, play deaf to whispering neighbors
at the Safeway, at the Chevron, at the . . .

Who goin' hire him when he get out?
I cup mama's weathered hands in mine, wounded birds trembling
God goin' take care, God goin' take care

Finding the right words I need
I move you in between *irresponsible*
and *irretrievable*. Close this book,
faithless, without memory

——————————— APRIL ———————————

Jean:

In my journal on March 21, 2008, I wrote: " 'Faithless, without memory.' This is what Christy gave me." Gave as in a gift. I had been watching the primaries with great intensity and the turmoil of the last eight years churned in me.

I took Christy's very personal story into our public nightmare: the events of the last years, the daily news of our failings, our crimes. My anger moved my fingers swiftly across the keyboard. Her "you," a brother, stuffed between the words "irresponsible" and "irretrievable," became our "he." You notice, this is my longest poem.

Faithless, without Memory

He didn't think about the after
or the before for that matter,

the time it didn't work,
the time all failed
the time we said, no, no, no,
never again.

No, he didn't think about that.

He just meddled and muddled
believing it would work
without plan
without knowledge
without loss
of our sons, our daughters,
our husbands, our wives,
our fathers, our mothers
our friends and acquaintances
names in the newspapers
names on the newscasts,
all 4273* of them
with more to come,

believing it could be done
without caring about the nameless
other sons and daughters, wives and husbands,
fathers and mothers, friends and acquaintances
whose names will not appear

with all the other
names to be written
on the marble waves
crushing the shores
of our remembrance.

* The number as of April 13, 2008.

Juliet:

Jean's poem in April ended with two lovely lines: crushing the shores/ of our remembrance. I was tempted to use the line above the ending line. I knew how water crushes the shores of memory. But I figured I better stick to the rules. So could I say anything "of our remembrance"? And whom could I include in the memory? Guilt is motivational so I thought of what I felt guilty about, over something remembered. My father's death had always haunted me, because I was callous, too selfish to see the signs that he was having a major heart infarction. I was too busy. I had a workshop to do. Painful as it was, I wanted to revisit the time and see how it would turn out in my reflections. At the end, the words "Until today/ I can't look into/ my memory of your eyes," was the truth, and it was truth revisited, with all of its foolishness, that finally spurred the writing of the poem.

Of Our Remembrances

We don't want to remember
what illuminates
the smallness of our hearts,
as on the morning
I saw you grip your knees
and break into a cold perspiration
that glistened on your face
like glycerin tears.

I wanted to be off,
out of the house,
and free of you—
the gnarly trees
of your age and fears,
of what you called
your "naughty" illness
that hindered my
run across the meadows.

Tucking the nitro tablet
under the log of your tongue,
I patted your hand
and released you
to your knot of pain.
I didn't wait to see—
was the pill working?

I had make-up to apply,
last minute notes to make,
the laundry to take out.
You called to me,
asked if I would massage
the pain in your back and arm.
"I don't have time," I said,
your howling eyes

following me out the door.

It was not the usual angina.
A flaw had sent you toppling.
Until today,
I can't look into
my memory of your eyes.

Ann:

I appreciated the last line of Juliet's poem in April, "my memory of your eyes." I thought of how anyone's eyes can change throughout the years. The greatest change in a person's eyes can be found when comparing childhood pictures and pictures as an adult. The poem is about a woman looking at pictures of herself when she was a child.

My Memory of Your Eyes

In album pages, I look
at thirty-year-old photos—
a skinny girl with short black hair
parted to the side
with a pin
securely placed
by her mother.

Her eyes hold
personality,
joy,
and unknowing.

I place my finger
on a photo
holding the girl's hand
glad that the camera
saved her eyes
when time
did not spin
and take everything.

These are the eyes of a girl
who is outside
smiling in the wind.

Christy:

I had complete writer's block for this line handed to me by Ann. Jean this month had pulled off a strong political statement, and Juliet in her usual grace came up with something that looked like it took months to fuss over. Ann's poem had a soft lingering sensibility and I could not do anything with the line. I had to turn to an old "Frankenstein" poem. I keep misshapen, half poems around. I may like a line or an image but know that it needs to be worked on. "Smile in the Wind" felt like this piece if I could work it. Although I was able to turn in something on time (I had to), I believe something about this piece failed. Something in the transitions, perhaps the second stanza could be pared down further. I hope that it conveyed a sense of devastation or surrender. As we don't get feedback on these, I still am not sure.

Smile in the Wind

Many years later,
he watches her sleep
the white hair, hollow skin, frozen
lines dwindling. He can't remember her laugh—

down at the boathouse by the Ala Wai
where dances were held every Saturday night.
So many parked cars they had to walk as far
as three blocks, but they could hear it
from that distance, the bass, the horns
taste the Latin notes as they held hands under
a copper sky hurrying toward the lighted pavilion.
Arthur Lyman's band wailing as they stepped
over conga beats towards the boys from McKinley
wearing pomade ducktails and tailored shirts.
Acknowledges them with a smirk, one arm around her
and the other raised high, a king over his court.
A good time, a lifetime, but there were also

accusations over lunch breaks, *How come you no answer
da phone when I call?* Every smile a threat
*Why he looking at you —you fucken whore.
Stay home, shit—* but baby needs
diapers and the electric is two months late
A difficult time, a lifetime, cutting him at all sides

No good Filipino boy—yeah da truck driva
fo Love's Bakery—get dat nice-looking hapa girl,
What she doing wit him? Too bad yeah.
Rusty nails through his shoe

He goes out to the rainy porch now, lights another
Marlboro. Glimpses her smile in the smoke
curling back in the wind. Takes another drag,
feels his tumor grow.

MAY

Jean:

My line, "the shores of our remembrance," sent everyone remembering something and Christy ends with someone smoking a cigarette (!), feeling his tumor grow.

What an awful title for a poem! So physical, so clinical. Having had to deal with tumors myself, I knew something about the experience. But I wanted it to be more than flesh. For many years I had thought about the power of naming and wanted to do something with the idea of how we can master our own world in our own way.

Later when I saw what Juliet had done with my "all that unknowing"—I was very pleased.

He Feels His Tumor Grow

That's what he calls it, that thing inside him
he doesn't know what.
Surely, the naming will tame it:
tumor, tumor. Then, it will
stop growing,
this feeling.
In him, on him, by him, with him . . .
he uses prepositions to make him think he knows.

>
> He doesn't.
> When did it start? It was always there,
> never there.
>
> He says his but doesn't know why.
> He doesn't possess it,
> even know it,
> but there it is,
> his;
> he feels it
> somewhere
> growing:
>
> all that unknowing.

Juliet:

Into May, "all that unknowing," and there were two poems about cancer, before mine, by Jean and Christy.

I am helping to care for my auntie. She is my favorite auntie. I go to see her every day at the hospital. She knows she is dying. Her family is having a hard time letting her go. This situation is what crowds my day. I am consumed by trying to help her die well.

I couldn't think about anything else, except visiting my auntie during this time, but I had a poem to write. It was natural that I carried over the theme. It was a difficult poem to write, because it was so emotional—the writing loose with too much to say, and I was pressured by time, work, and death. My first draft (a rare one saved) was not going anywhere. It didn't even follow Jean's last line. Where was I going to take it? The first draft:

> The storm clouds hit.
> The moon in Pleiades
> sets in the East.
> It continued raining into the morning,
> and you were still alive, covering
> but the distance.
>
> By her light touch,
> the hospice nurse awakens you
> to check your blood pressure,

and still earthbound
you look at the time.

After several other drafts like the one above, I finally settled on using Jean's last line to form the first line and go right into the poem. In the end, the writing of this poem, about what was happening in the hospital room, worked as a lavage. It was grandly therapeutic. It was self-centered and selfish, overindulgent, and yes, I admit, solipsistic, but boy did it feel good!

All That Unknowing

of what lay beneath the glassy surface
of the sea before you,
made you want to dive,
deep,
into its dark-blue secrets
and trapped air.

You have finally reached bottom.
Now, you are heading up,
as if in an unwinding
of your life's journey.
So your dying
comes as no surprise,
except to those who thought you'd live
forever. They deceptively cling to you,
as they would a life raft,
and in the end, to life itself.

You need this time
to grieve for yourself,
times you fetched
the morning paper from the stoop,
turned over the frying rice,
or helped your daughter with her sweater.
All life's work.
But to them this grieving means
that you are giving up the sky
or that burst of moonlight above you.
They make you feel guilty
for having lost your hat to the wind,
for not trying harder to beat your illness.

But I see it in your eyes.
You are holding onto nothing.
You are finding
that there's a certain
grace and relief
in acknowledging
your fatalistic move up
toward the light-flushed surface,
as when you first dove in,
at birth,
and shattered the water.

Ann:

I was excited about the title "Shattered Water" for May since there could be many stories linked to water breaking. In this scene, the character shatters her reflection, but she also notices how her image is whole again after the rock dives to the bottom. Her whole image gives her strength to retrace her path and return to the sound of crying dogs. I debated whether I should end the poem with "and weathered houses" or "She could still hear the dogs crying." I decided that the main character should hear the dogs again, so I ended the poem with that last line. I kept thinking of Christy and hoped for the best.

Shattered Water

She ran past the weathered houses,
fenced gardens, and crying dogs.
Air escaped from her throat,
and it was hard to breathe.
As her legs teared with sweat,
her eyes saw water running
through a canal.

She picked up a rock,
threw it at her reflection,
and shattered the water.

In the water,
pieces of herself dispersed
and reassembled.

She stared at her image.
Then, she turned around and walked
past the fenced gardens
and weathered houses.

She could still hear the dogs crying.

Christy:

I couldn't believe Ann gave me this line. Are you kidding me? Hear the dogs crying? What is that? Okay. okay, okay. Time to make something out of nothing. And it did come to me, while listening to NPR, the story of a woman from Africa. I loved her voice, the depth of it, the gravelly tones, the different imagery. "Hear the Dogs Crying" was a completely different poem in its first write through. It was of an African village, and the landscape was the Serengeti. It had also contained a line in it, an African proverb, *Usisafire nyota ya mwenzio*, which I love. It means, *Don't set sail using someone else's star*, an admonition to follow your own path. I wondered how well it would go over, since I was writing for *Bamboo Ridge*, a local journal. Would the audience get it? I know you are supposed to write poetry for yourself, but then again, if no one gets it, you should keep it to yourself. I wrote this poem again, Hawaiian style, different imagery, different catalyst. I showed both poems to a couple of friends who related better to the Hawaiian version. So it is that version that is posted for the month of May. I have kept the original version though, as I believe it to be the stronger one, and am submitting it to a mainland journal contest. Yeah, two poems for the price of one.

National Public Radio

A recording of her voice,
an old woman's voice full of gravel and lead steeped through
the car radio. It had a lion's mane
dressed in robes of dull orange which decidedly
lingered behind like a bridal veil,
pulling on the S's, snagging the T's.

She spoke of her village in Africa; gathering plantains,
crooked politicians, and snake bite remedies.

In the distance you could almost hear
the dogs crying, the kerosene tin pot crackle.

Nostalgic for something I never knew,
I feel a drum beat pulse inside me,
beaded rattles shaking me raising me
pushing me till I leap—

Emerge as a curve in the Serengeti.
I move past the kopjes,
past the acacia trees
towards thatched huts where children
home from school, kick up clouds
of dust, singing women wearing colorful kanga
light firewood under black pots for dinner
*Usisafire nyota ya mwenzio**

I have tomatoes and fish from the market sistah
Have I been gone that long?
and some bones for the dogs to stop their crying
I have not been gone that long.
I am listening for your stories on this endless land
Have I been gone that long?
the skies have carried me back—No—
I have not been gone that long

**Usisafire nyota ya mwenzio*, proverb: "Don't set sail using someone else's star," an admonition to follow your own path, your own destiny.

Hear the Dogs Crying

A recording of her voice, an old woman's voice
full of gravel and lead steeped through
the car radio. She spoke of gathering limu
visitors on ships, and dusty roads in Waiʻanae.
In the distance you could almost hear
the dogs crying, the mullet wriggling in the fish bag

Nostalgic for a tutu I never knew,
I feel the ocean pulse inside me
waves rolling over, pushing me till I leap
from this car through the congested H-1
across the noise and ashen sky

emerge beneath the rains in Nuʻuanu.
I move past the fresh water ponds
past the guava trees towards homes
with flimsy tin roofs where

my father, already late for school,
races up Papakōlea with a kite made
of fishing twine. Framed in a small kitchen
window, tutu scrapes the meat from awa skin
for dinner tonight, wipes her hands on
old flour bags for dish cloths.
She is already small and wants to forget
I may be too late—

I have tomatoes and onion from the market, tutu,
my hand is out, my plate is empty
and some bones for the dogs to stop their crying
do you know my name?
I am listening for your stories to call me in
my hand is out, my plate is empty
for your stories to show me the way
tutu, do you know my name?

JUNE

Jean:

Christy's "Do you know my name?" was very appropriate. Remembering names had become a nuisance to me these past few years. That younger people complained of the same affliction was of no comfort. I always felt superior to other teachers because I could learn the names of all my students after one day of class. Now, it was taking more time and I was losing the names of people I had known for years.

This had become a subject of discussion for my sister, my mother, and me. More frustrating is that my mother, who is eighty-eight years old, can remember names better than I.

I wrote this poem in my journal on May 21, 2008. It came to me in one fell swoop.

Do You Know My Name?

It just irked her no end when she couldn't pull out the name that should have matched the face in front of her.

She had in the past been able to grab a sliver of a syllable,
a letter like an "M" that led to Martha or Milly or
some clue that pulled out a name.
When no letter came, she'd look at the face
and went through the alphabet: a, b, c, d, e . . .
until some sound from inside came out through
her tongue: Emma?
No, not Emma.
She waited for that feeling of relief, a confirmation
that she could remember.

So, do you know my name? asked
the face looking from the mirror.

Juliet:

Early June. I have to write a poem on the road. I couldn't conceive how I was going to do it all, let alone write a poem. I wanted to ask Darrell, "Hey, can I come back to this a later time?" But my mother's presence kicked in. I heard her voice: "You have to be responsible." Needless to say, I was having a meltdown. I was tired. I called Wing Tek and threatened to quit. I told him that I couldn't do it—just couldn't. While diplomatic as he always is, he never gave me an out. He didn't say it, but I heard the "No ways!" under his calmness. "Ways!" I wanted to say.

A confession: ever since I was a child, I feared, no hated, Sunday nights, because that meant school the next day, and I hadn't finished my homework. Sunday was the best but worst day of the week. The old inadequacies haunted me. I was reaching Sunday night with no poem to submit. For the first time in the series, I went on the computer cold and started writing. I had to write something, after all, and I was surprised. For once, I was lucky. I knew I couldn't do this all of the time, having tried it before, but this one time it worked. Not the best poem, for this process seldom works for me, because I need the time to write by hand for a decent poem to evolve, but, after it was done, it was adequate.

The Face Looking from the Mirror

Isn't rounder
or stronger.
Not a face to be afraid
of in its song.
It is kinder,
more gentle,
glow-softened
by petticoat-white
lights, ruffled
as oncidium orchids.

. . . stares out in longing
for a simple kiss,
the precision of nesting tables,
the pin-wheel whites,
along the walkway
that brushed her skirts
as she walked by
and passed through sorrow,
of her life
and you.
The sky in the mirror
is blue, the grass green
and you want
to bring her flowers,
write her a poem
before she leaves.

Ann:

Since I wrote poems regarding death, life, and identity for the previous months, I wanted my June poem to be different. At the time, I received good news: I will be teaching at Kapiʻolani Community College in the fall semester. I was excited and looked forward to planning my syllabi for English classes. In the poem, I wanted to include the simplicity of looking forward to an upcoming profession with freshness and hope. The blue flowers in the poem are blue daze flowers, which bloom in the morning and live for a day. Although each flower's life is short, the blue daze continues to bloom many times.

Before She Leaves

Blue flowers open
near the cement pathway
and she walks down
porch steps.

The sky is lovely
as she breathes in
and walks to the car.

She has books to read
and lesson plans to prepare
for her first classes in the fall.

Before she leaves,
she looks up
to see birds flying
from the clouds.

Christy:

This poem was conceived in Aotearoa. I had just returned from there with my halau and the experience was heavy in my heart. The first two stanzas are a retelling of the Maori creation myth whereby Father Sky (Rangi) and Mother Earth (Papa) are torn apart by their children. "From the clouds" was the perfect lead in for me to relive this piece of their culture and tie it in to the modern day workings of what I know so well, the life and death aspects of working in a hospital.

From the Clouds

Father Sky looked down
on all the beauty of Mother Earth
the hills, the valleys, then clasped her tightly.
So close was the embrace, their children;
the winds, the forests, the birds
only knew darkness

On their knees and shoulders, the children
pushed them, no—ripped them apart so they
could live in the light. Father Sky grieved much.

Grandma grieves much.

Another week of that breathing tube
for you Grandpa, another week of bloody
brown urine, beeping monitors and repentant nurses
"I'm so sorry, so sorry."

We go to the chapel to pray, on our knees
she to the god of medicine, and I—
I dig my knees deep into this church pew, dig beneath
the dirty shag rug through the floor boards till
my knees rip the stitches binding us here
in this endless maze of tubes and feeble doctors.
On my shoulders I hold back Grandma's tears
your wedding vows and first home in Pālolo valley.
The small things so heavy now, I carry too;
your calloused hands,
the smell of sardines and chili pepper water,
mending old fishing nets in the early morning.

I pray to cut the anchor of your sinking vessel
I pray you catch the tail of the wind
I pray a small light to lead you from this darkness

JULY

Jean:

I noticed that the links of June were very personal—not that the others weren't—but this batch seemed even more so. Christy's "from this darkness" led me to my own personal story. Actually, it was my husband who told me about his mother who had healed people in their Kohala neighborhood. My own grandmother had done the same in Kōloa, so somehow those figures merged into my mother, and I into the child.

The iridescent bugs actually came from my memories of Sheridan behind the Shingon Temple, the space now occupied by Keʻeaumoku Street. I remember sitting on the outside steps in the evening trying to catch glowing green bugs that hovered overhead.

From this Darkness

I see a small light
green and glowing.
It moves from side to side
like the sagelampu I carried
for you, Mama.
You said,
"Quick get the lamp, Tanouesan has a high fever."
I held the lamp in front of us and the light
would zigzag along the dirt path
in rhythm with our footfalls.
Your healing cups would clink in time
with the crunch of dirt and small stones under our feet.
We were alone except for frogs croaking in the dark
and the iridescent
bugs
buzzing along with us.

Juliet:

Summer. July. A bit of respite from school. "Buzzing Along with Us"—I had to think about this one. What buzzes along with us? In my thinking, it was memory—that repository of memory that haunts you—good, bad, or indifferent. Once I decided that this is what I was going to write about, writing the poem wasn't too bad. I was free of schoolwork, and I could concentrate on writing in a leisurely manner.

Buzzing Along with Us

are your companions in life—
your memories—
that can spring out of nowhere.
Take you to a childhood afternoon
or light a mountain trail
you once walked—
the same light attenuated by bamboo,
swaying in the wind's coming—
where a fall off the precipice
meant no returning
to the porch shaded
by the jacaranda.

Or, a sudden face
you had not thought of in years
may flash before you,
young as you saw it last,
but wouldn't recognize, today.
They take your hands,
never let them go.
They make no neat patterns in your mind.
They may play tricks
or impress upon you,
a longing,
for the times she wore
the water-lily dress
that floated around her in a cloud,
cupped the white ginger in her hands,
or dreamed of banquets
when she no longer could eat.
Even that, once more.
Warm or chilling,
they stay with you
like a quiet child might,
or a noisy one,
but always at your side without apology,
waiting to take you down
the street you ran on
with your sad old dog
or the wobbly bicycle wheel
you rolled with a stick
in the spindle of summer
that unraveled the threads of your life.
They bring up matters
that send sentimental tears
down your cheeks;
feed into your old heartaches.
And oftentimes, in your recollections,
you pass them off
to your children
without ever meaning to be cruel.

Ann:

All of my previous *renshi* poems were in Standard English, and I wished for a chance to write a poem in Pidgin. As I was waiting for the last line of Juliet's poem, I thought of scenes I could write in Pidgin. I remembered Biology class in high school with a scene that included mice. I hoped Juliet's last line would somehow be related to the topic I wanted to write about. When I finally saw her last line, I was pleasantly surprised; it was the title I wanted for my poem, so I started writing the entire scene. As I wrote it, I realized that there are many who wish the best for others similar to the main character in this poem, but sometimes the results are the opposite from what was intended.

Without Meaning to Be Cruel

One teacha asked me if I wanted fo be his teacha's aide fo Biology class.
My classmates said was good fo be one teacha's aide
cuz you just help and das it.
Not like you one student in class and gotta do class work.
Was my senior year and I had most of da credits fo graduate
so I decided fo be his teacha's aide.

I ran errands fo him and did stuffs like enter grades into his grade book.
Layda on, he told me dat dea was going be one teacha fo replace him
cuz he got one nodda job.

Da new teacha was one lady who look like she just graduated college.
One day, she brought one glass tank wit white mice inside.
She had to leave fo get someting, and I was in charge of da class.
Everybody was studying, so I looked inside da tank.
I saw one mouse go by da odda mouse.
Look like da mouse was pulling off da odda mouse's hairs.
I dunno if dis normal. I wanted da pulling fo stop,
so I started poking da mouse wit one stick.
Da mouse neva stop, so I kept poking um.

Everybody gathered around da tank.
Layda, da mouse finally stopped pulling.
I was still holding da stick.
I shoulda told everybody fo go back to dea desks, but I neva.
I wanted fo make sure da mouse neva pick on da odda mouse again.
I kept poking.
Da mouse's head started fo twitch.

Wen da teacha came back, everybody went back to dea desks.
She asked da class wat happened.
Everybody looked at me and neva say nothing.
She started da lesson as I looked inside da tank.
Why da mouse gotta keep twitching laidat?

I hoped da mouse would stop twitching next class
but it neva.

Every class, I look da tank and wish I neva do wat I did.
Da teacha saw da mouse, and I no can look her in da eye
wen she asked me wat happened.

Christy:

This month's poems were a good batch. I noticed that both Juliet and Ann had longer poems this month. I'm usually the one with the long-winded voice. I wanted something compact and more formal, a change from how I had been writing before. "She asked" was a complete gimme. I could write about anything. As it turns out, a love poem arose. The only one to date I have ever written.

She Asked

What to give you?

The black bird or the perfect arc
it made while flying upward over

green cypress reminding me of
Roman coliseums and grander things

than this three story walk-up.
Perhaps a moment, which expanded

and breathed when I saw
fragile translucent star blossoms

a field of them blanketing the lawn
that one day will be our home.

And I wasn't afraid.
A song, I'll give you a song

to sing to the rocks we will use
to fill that defunct septic tank.

They'll carry that tune to the
wooden beams of our future,

hammered together by hands that pray
with gratitude for all we do not know.

AUGUST

Jean:

"With gratitude for all we do not know" gave me a lot of trouble, because I couldn't at that moment think of being grateful for not knowing. As a matter of fact, ignorance irks me, though this is stupid. How can any human being know everything? Now I can think of instances when ignorance is a blessing. But as a title for a poem, "all we do not know" did nothing for me. However, it started me thinking. There are so many things I do not know; I started with the biggest.

> **All We Do Not Know**
>
> That remains a mystery to me:
>
> the nature of dark matter—MACHOs or Massive Compact Halo
> Objects, WIMPs or Weakly Interacting Massive Particles and neutrinos,
> those billion to one particles
> for every proton and electron in the universe,
>
> the nature of dark energy—cosmological constant, scalar fields
> energizing the accelerating expansion of the universe
>
> the reality of hyperspace in ten dimensions making possible time
> travel on the warping and rippling of space
>
> the promise of superstrings which will unite stars and galaxies with
> the molecules
> of my own DNA
>
> makes me hungry
>
> for the big and small of it,
> for the fast and slow of it
> for the hot and cold of it;
> for the ins and outs
>
> of the whys and wherefores.

Juliet:

Oh my, my, my. The next last line—actually an august sounding line—high fallutin' line—kind of old-fashioned line—reminded me of a Shakespearean line—and it had me stumped. I didn't know what it *really* meant. *For real kine, but sorry, I hated the line. I Googled. I Wikipedia-ed. What was I going to do? After pondering the meaning—my time almost ova just trying to figure out the doggone meaning. Den I sorta got it: reason, an explanation. In the meantime, I kept on getting it confused with* whereof. *Stoopid. Not whereof—wherefores.* WHEREFORES—*you got it?*

Again, I went on my computer, cold, with time at my heels. "We ponder/ pull them out/ as from a magician's hat." It was just the feeling I had. While the poem didn't turn out as well as I had hoped, it was done. I posted it, barely on time. I didn't obsess. I moved on.

I let it go like a kite.

Of the Whys and Wherefores

we ponder.
Pull them out,
as from a magician's hat.

Small at first,
the questions—
like the easy trick
of making a quarter appear
from the petal of a child's ear
that makes him smile and run
to his mother and say, "Look what I've got!"
Of spouting a lifeline of blood-red scarves
from hands that we can swear were empty
the last time we looked,
the answers more cloudy.

How are we going to pull this off,
produce a dove from a sleeve
a hand or head,
another then another—a small flock?
An illusionist will tell you
that handling what is real
takes more care.

But in the end, it's the disappearing
acts that hold our attention.
The mystery of it all.
We want to know why
we can't see the wind
or where meteor showers
come from, where they go,
giving us the perfect
opportunity to ask—
why we're here, then not.

Ann:

I read the last line, "why we're here, then not," and I had no idea what to write about. At first, I wrote a poem about a mynah bird at a bus stop.

Why We're Here

At the bus stop,
a mynah was dead
on the cement
behind the bench.

A lady saw the small bird
and gently moved it with a twig
flipped it from side to side
until the mynah's legs moved.

She told me sometimes
we just need to move them
to bring them back.

On Sunday, I decided to write another poem. I had visited a pond earlier, and I wrote down observations of the animals I saw. Maybe I could use the notes I wrote earlier for a poem. I looked at the last line again. I had difficulty using the entire last line, but I could write a poem about characters at a pond with the title "We're Here." I included my observations at the pond with two characters in a relationship that will be ending. If you read the poem one way, the narrator sounds as if she wishes time could rewind and she could stay with him. The poem read another way signals that she wishes he were gone and the next day would come soon.

We're Here

We return to the pond
where a koi slaps the water
and a turtle dives in.
As water falls into the pond,
I hear you breathe.

A dragonfly passes
and a sparrow hops
through the weeds.
As we sit in the shade,
I hear you breathe.

You will leave soon
and summer is ending.
As I hold you tight,
I hear you breathe.

The sky dims
and the wind is cool.
As we walk to the car,
I hold my breath
wishing it was morning.

Christy:

You know those kinds of exercises they give you to write a poem? Well, this one came from that kind of exercise, trying to write about a work of art. What struck me most about Kamehameha I's portrait was its small stature. This in contrast to the great aura of warrior and king that his name projects. I had been reading Tim O'Brien's works about the Vietnam War and was inspired to write about a battle, and to capture the fierce movement of it.

It Was Morning

(on viewing Choris's portrait of Kamehameha I)

It was morning when I first saw you
on a slim side wall where
someone might absentmindedly flip
a light switch. Not the center of the gallery
with guards flanking you, cordoned off
by velvet ropes. Instead

you are housed in a small common frame
constricted by a fading red vest.
Your gray hair creates a halo effect;
a pious merchant, an aging choirboy. Impostor.

Where are you, my king?

You are there a shadow on the horizon
amidst a fleet of ten, a hundred, a thousand,
engulfing as the waves that surround this island,
seated on the ama, eyes perched on the shores of Waikīkī.
You are there in the tall grass of Nuʻuanu,
sun gleaming off your thighs, your chest.
Moʻo skin helmets your face allowing
only the black pupil widening to be seen,
your calloused hand holding back the spear
anxious for the release. You are there
in the first clashes of muscle and teeth,
salt sweat drawing light onto your skin
as the ʻelepaio shrieks in the branches above.
Your spear tip pushes father and brother to the edge
Imua! Imua! and 400 more leap like mullets
into stony nets waiting below.

A pact of silence has been made by the bones left behind,
I go to those pastures to break it. I go to listen
to find you, my king. Too many have been misled by this canvas.

SEPTEMBER

Jean:

Once again I was struck by very personal stories written by the other poets. I struggled with this one but thought I'd try something personal.

The word "canvas" left me at a loss. "Misled by this canvas" was even worse. I could think of nothing and didn't want to return to the canvas of paintings. I thought of things made of canvas. It was awful. The only single thread in my memory was the canvas of my father's old working belt that really functioned as a bag. It was a kind of tool holder that he, a carpenter, wore around his waist. He'd come home with his belt and his clothes all covered with sawdust. I miss the sawdust.

Canvas

An old canvas bag tucked in between tattered boxes
lying on the floor of the storage room crisscrossed
by cobwebs:
I'm selling the family house.

The canvas is yellow, splotched with brown hues
covered with dust from the ages.
Whose canvas bag?
I untie the knot that holds the heavy contents:
standard sized hammer, medium chisel, a few
five-inch nails.

The rough surface of the canvas, the smell of lost time
scrape away the years and I see my father
coming home from work
tired, but happy to see us, his daughters.
We climb over him and empty his pant cuffs.
The sawdust of the day spills out.
It's like finding gold.

Juliet:

For September's poem, I changed the last line, "It's like finding gold," to "It was like finding gold" and proceeded to write my poem. It was one year ago, exactly, that I had been in Kyoto. Visiting Higashi Hongwanji after a day of studying, I came across a hair rope on display. Looking back, I thought about how hair was like gold for these women who cut it to make the hair ropes to help build a temple that had burned down in the 19th century. I wasn't and am not much into sacrifice (except, perhaps, in writing a year's worth of *renshi*), and I reflected on how these women must have felt and how I felt when I saw the braided hair.

It Was Like Finding Gold

After the fire,
an act of devotion.

Thousands of women cut
their hair for the thigh-thick braids
of hair ropes that lifted
the heavy spruce beams
taken from medieval loam.
Ordinary ropes would not have been able
to lift and have these beams loom over
worshippers in the Grand Amida Hall
after the rebuilding of the Eastern Temple.
Of high gloss—
ebony but gold, more—
the hair ropes lifted the burden
of the women's attachment.
As I looked into the glass
display case of their sacrifice,
I touched my own hair
and thought of hair
that lifted the beams
up toward the open rafters,
up toward the stars
and up toward the moon.
Upward and outward
toward nothing
and the uncreated.

Ann:

I read the last line, "and the uncreated," and I thought about all the ideas that haven't been born and the challenge to create. There is a need to be receptive to ideas while waiting for words, sounds, and images to click. It was September, and honestly, I was tired, a bit burnt out, and I felt like I was in the beginning stage of a cold. At the time, I could smell my mother's cooking from the kitchen. There's nothing like the smell of miso soup when you are ill. It's comforting, and it made me want to persevere and get this poem done.

The Uncreated

She lies on her bed and stares at the ceiling
while her body is heavy from a cold.

The smell of miso soup and warm squash
cooked in dashi, shoyu, and sugar

comes from the kitchen.

As she looks at her empty notepad,
she sees the clock's rotating hand.

She stares at the uncreated
until words assemble and sounds connect.
The room fills with stories.

Christy:

Another road trip poem, this time just to Seattle to visit a friend. The Frida reference, as well as the Dominican Republic images, came courtesy a bookstore where my friend and I spent the afternoon. (The name of the store is escaping me now, but it wasn't a big chain deal. An old-fashioned bookstore near the harbor with wooden floors, a cozy feel and a poetry section to die for.) Just a conscious stream of thought which took off with images like Frida's painting, "The Suicide of Dorothy Hale," which is a reference to the woman falling from a New York City skyscraper. I combined it with the imagery found in Junot Diaz's *The Brief Wondrous Life of Oscar Wao*. This led to memories—snapshots in my mind—which tied the tragedies together. It wound up with a mongoose in Waimānalo. Who would have thought a mongoose could be an oracle?

The Room Fills With

images like a Frida Kahlo painting;
a woman falling from a New York city skyscraper
bloodied with eyes wide open, images
of brutality in a Dominican Republic cane field
against large breasted young girls shining
in their last breath, all of it for love, love, love.
Images of you and I at the cafe where I learned to like coffee
poring over frivolous details to you and you
learned women were much better weak better
than they could ever be strong in all their tender parts.
See the flutter of her dress
see the dust rising from the field
see me look up with butterfly lids
pregnant with tears folded over like proteas, descending

from such heights into the *shsk shsk*
of Waimānalo brush and the wild eyes of a mongoose staring
out at us that night when the moon was full and our hearts were full with
the yellow eyes of a lion
trying to warn me.

OCTOBER

Jean:

In my journal I wrote: "'Trying to warn me.' Tough line—think of Cassandra, warning labels/signs, don't want to be predictable."

I stared at the words "Trying to warn me." Nothing. I had to scour my mind to find instances when warnings were given. I searched the Internet. I despaired. I hoped that staring at the words would bring inspiration. Nothing. I had 70 hours. On TV I saw the poet laureate of Portland talking about poems inscribed on stones laid out in a park commemorating the Japanese interned in camps during WWII. That was something worth warning about. I wrote something and went to sleep.

The next morning I had another idea, one about the fantail filefish I often thought about, after I saw so many at Brennecke Beach on Kaua'i. I read somewhere that they portend the death of a king when seen in abundance. I wrote that poem.

I compared the two. I liked both. The dilemma, which to choose. Maybe I could end with the same last line.

The one not chosen:

Trying to Warn Me

They were strewn upon the beach
so many as to cover the sand.
Rotting, stinking
with more in the water.

Adorned with black dots on yellow

outlined in blue starting from the mouth
to the tail which turns orange and black.
If you see one, you'll never forget it.
Now they surround me in the waters of
Brennecke Beach.

Hawaiians say great numbers of ʻuwī ʻuwī
portend the death of a chief.
When that happened, there would be
hell to pay.

I chose the other one because of the potential of new concentration camps.

Trying to Warn Me

They warned them about us, about me.
We were one of them.
Not to be trusted, they said.

Don't talk so loud, she said.
Speak English, she said.
So I went to my room and hid my dolls with wobbly heads.

They'll be coming, don't you doubt it, they'll be coming
and we'll be blamed
because of the curve of our nose,
the slant of our eyes.
Mark my words,
there'll be hell to pay.

Juliet:

As October rolled around, I began to see the light at the end of the tunnel and the work we did felt great—the variety and the difference in the voices, wonderful. Jean ended her poem that month with "there'll be hell to pay." By this time the stock market was falling precipitously, and I was thinking how grateful I was despite the downturn in our lives. I could live small. I didn't need fancy things—not that I ever did—so I was okay. I had my health, I had a decent job, I had a roof over my head, I had my cat, I had my son, I had good friends. This was the point of my poem. Who could want anything more? Truly.

There'll Be Hell to Pay

And we are paying,
the Dow falling
precipitously in the shale of greed.

Now I have portion control.
My husband grows thinner.
I divvy up the stone potatoes, stone carrots.
I go around to turn off unnecessary lights.
We eat in, take home-lunch to work,
five-minute showers, search for black
currents and unplug computers.
We eat no fat and dream lean.
Teeth against the meat bone.
We do whatever it takes,
as we watch the rock of our pensions
disappear over the cliff.
Where did it all go?
"To money heaven," you say.
"Just to money heaven."

I go outside to look
up at the sky.
I see that it is all there—
the pebbles of clouds,
the ambient crystals of light,
a blue-rock sky
that's not bad
to have or need.

Ann:

During the week, I was wondering what I could write about regarding something I had or something I needed. I didn't know what the poem was going to be about. Then, literally, there was a power outage. It was perfect timing. When I was younger, I thought electricity was something that we had but didn't need since generations before us survived without it. Now, I realize our dependency on it.

To Have or Need

My battery alarm clock buzzed at 4:30 a.m.,

and I walked toward my parents' voices
as the radio talked about the power outage
and we listened with flashlights.

I brushed my teeth, put on makeup,
and changed clothes in dim light.
Then I carried a bag containing
papers I graded the night before
grateful that there was power yesterday.

I reversed out of the driveway with caution
and measured the distance
between car headlights
as I crossed the intersection.

There were rows of lights on the freeway,
and I drove along with everyone
trying to forget the inconvenience
depending on lights to guide my way.

Christy:

A lighter poem this month, of the things that guided me, shaped me. A celebration of living here in Hawaiʻi.

Depending on Lights to Guide My Way

Thanks to the local bradas, playing uke Friday night,
anybody's backyard, Pauoa valley. The clink
of their green bottles drifting up to moths
dancing in the porch light guiding my way.

And to Nana who comes faithfully
to early mass every Sunday,
dressed in low-heeled square-toed shoes,
genuflecting before a mosaic of apostles
in stained glass light guiding my way.

There are others; Japanese cops in Korean bars,
Chinatown butchers chopping char siu,
the bedridden in Leahi who outlive their children.

As I set sail on this moonless life,
I go over a riverbed of stones casting off
sparks as we touch, brief lights

illuminating the long journey ahead.
I keep an eye out for the fires.

NOVEMBER

Jean:

Christy gave me "keep an eye out for the fires," which I tried to work into the poem I had already decided to write. This was the first time I had started a poem without having Christy's line. I had something to say.

"The time of the great healing has come" was the line I wanted to use. It was the Sunday before the elections, and I was pulling for Barack Obama.

The line turned into "Let the great healing begin."

> **The Fires**
>
> The flames have leapt from point to point
> unabated:
> first our eyes
> then our ears,
> into our hearts
> into our spleens,
> our insides
> scorched.
>
> We fight each other.
> Fear blinds us.
>
> Put the fires out.
> They have burned for eight years.
>
> Let the great healing begin.

Juliet:

It was election time, and the November series of poems reflected this event. Barack Obama filled our thoughts and good wishes for the country. For Jean, she was well rid of Bush fires and tactics and was ready to "let the great healing begin." I talked about Obama's grandmother, when she was dying, and a grandson's visit. Ann's poem exulted his winning the election and Christy's his move to the White House. It was so interesting how the poems evolved in this manner. It wasn't planned, but I marveled at how it all fell into place. I was feeling pretty good about our lives, and yes, about the *renshi* project.

Let the Great Healing Begin

He is here
to visit his dying grandmother.
She lives in an apartment
building a few blocks away
from where we live,
and where he spent his childhood,
walking to and from school
or his part-time job, scooping ice cream.

Early in the morning
while on our daily walk in the hush,
we go past the building and vow—
should we but glimpse his sorrow—
to run away
and release him to his privacy.

No one's around.
The TV vans that cover every moment
of his life sit quietly in the church
parking lot across the street.
We walk back home
and on the way,
stop beneath an 'opiuma tree
that sheds its petals in the coming light
to the shine of tears.

Ann:

This month, there was a trend. Everyone was writing about someone in politics. When I read the last line, "to the shine of tears," I was reminded of the audience in Chicago listening to Barack Obama's speech after he won the presidential election. Obama represented hope for so many. Within the last few months, everything was going downhill, and people talked about the possibility of the economy going into a depression. Many listened intently to Obama's speech, and I was grateful for this opportunity to have a poem about Obama's historic inauguration.

Shine of Tears

On November 4, 2008,
a man, unlike predecessors before him,
walks to a podium in Chicago
to address a nation
with his acceptance speech.

In a shine of tears, some remember:
falling stock market
housing market
credit crisis
war.

The president-elect walks on stage
with his wife and two daughters.

There's a lot to accomplish
as Barack Obama and his family
prepare to move into the White House.

Christy:

I cursed all the women preceding me this month: Curse you, Jean, Juliet, and Ann! How could you all write about Obama?! I felt cornered into writing a poem about Obama, not only because all three had chosen to write about him, but I was given the line "prepare to move into the White House." There really isn't too much you can do with that. It's not that I had a problem with Obama—but forced creativity on a subject is *soooo* un-American. Where was my freedom? Aaugh. I challenged myself not to write about Obama, to see if I was a good enough poet. Then I challenged myself to write about Obama, because in truth, that was going to be tricky. I like to write poems with a familiar background, areas or feelings that I can relate to. Obama was outside of my personal zone, what could I say about him? I thought and thought. I read Merwin and thought some more. I decided to go with the Obama idea; after all, I was excited to have him as our new leader and we actually did have something very personal in common, growing up in Hawai'i. That would be our tie.

Prepare to Move into the White House

I imagine you would take us with you,
perhaps rolled up in a Persian rug
or tucked in hidden pockets of your luggage
carrying white shirts, socks, and underwear.

There is no need to take us out
right away, no need to show us around.
Forget about us as you do your spine or spleen.

But when old chains begin to rattle
in your mind, or on the lips of suits
lining red carpeted hallways
that no longer seem new to you

we will be there; trade winds twisting
down the Ko'olau, fragrant fallen mangos,
nests of salt. Let us offer you respite, let us
be a toe hold in the craggy wall you climb
treading a new path to a new country.

Let us remind you of when hope
was measured in pocket change
after a long day of body surfing—
just enough for shaved ice and the bus ride home.

DECEMBER

Jean:

November was amazing, like a symphony holding all its parts together, changing but retaining a theme. I loved the development, the flow, and then Christy's finish. Just perfect. I thought she hit the right notes for his entrance into the White House.

The line "just enough for shaved ice and the bus ride home" brought to mind the photo of him and his daughters eating shave ice. (Christy and I discussed the shaved and the shave. As you can see, we chose different forms of the word.) I, too, wanted to let him know, as Christy had, that we will support him through the bad as well as the good, through his triumphs and his failures. So how to put that in a poem that starts with "Shave ice" or "Just enough for shave ice"?

No, that would be too indulgent. Enough of Obama. I knew that this was my last poem for this *renshi*. There needed to be a marker to end this year of writing poetry with Juliet, Ann and Christy. I tried again.

Just Enough Shave Ice

To bring a strawberry smile to my lips
To cool the heat off my bones
To calm the clamor in me
raised through these months
of deadlines and forced creation.
It's just reward for the end of this adventure
with three strangers who've become fellow
laborers in ridging gaps

But I rejected this poem, because I needed to say something in pidgin. After all, BR has been its champion. I don't often write in pidgin and I have been told that you cannot mix pidgin with regular English. So that's what I wanted to do; I do that all the time in speech.

On this weekend we were celebrating 30 years of *Bamboo Ridge* at the Hale Koa Hotel. The theme was "Not Pau Yet!" How prophetic! I got the feeling that the BR gang still had more to do and, miraculously enough, energy to continue. So I put no period at the end of my poem, which is not my best, but it will do.

Thanks to this commentary, I can include my rejects, which I didn't want to throw away.

And thanks to the instigators and supporters who read the proofs and made suggestions: Eric, who pointed out the obvious title and read the manuscript, and Darrell, who did all that plus pulled the strings. A very special thanks to Wing Tek for his many phone calls during which he suggested summaries, made cogent comments about the essay, and gave me insight into the whole enterprise. He also revealed the secret that I was the "last resort"! My thanks to Julie Ushio for helping with the final touches of my essay. And for our CD, many thanks to Sammie Choy and Jason Taglianetti.

Most of all, my heartfelt gratitude to the poets who said yes: Juliet S. Kono, Ann Inoshita, and Christy Passion. It would not have been possible without you.

Just Enough Shave Ice

For make my lips red like strawberry
For cool me off and calm me down
afta all dis and all dat

Just enough hope for me
to think that yes we can
do this
and do that
with all we have
or don't have

Just enough time for finish my poem
For da dis of da dat

Just enough space to write
All these thirty years
We did this
We did that

And no,
We not pau yet

Juliet:

My last poem to write. As I looked over the past year, I was so honored to be part of this wonderful group of women, with such wonderful voices. I was amazed that we managed to pull it off for one year. While I don't believe that I would ever do it again, it was a lesson, even at my age, about responsibility, deadlines, frustration, discipline, and hope. Why hope? Because I needed the line for my next poem, and sometimes hope was all I had going for me—in hopes that the line would suddenly appear, not be that difficult, and that I would be able to make something of it!

When Jean wrote the last line for her last poem—"not pau yet"—my heart sank. I thought to myself it couldn't be true. They couldn't be thinking of going on. I didn't know about the others, but for me it was over. I was all pau! (Nevertheless, I do hope that others may be inspired to take this *renshi* up for themselves.)

My special thanks to Jean, Ann, Christy, Darrell, Sammie Choy, Jason Taglianetti, and all the others who supported us. I learned a lot from it, and thank you Wing for suggesting that I be part of this project....

Not Pau Yet

My father's interrogative,
"What, not pau yet? How come?"
was always followed
by my mother's declarative,
"No, not pau yet,"
followed by my unvoiced imperative,
"Do it yourself, den!"

My reflection of these moments
of a man who did nothing around the house,
is accompanied by ripples of pity
for his pools of impatience,
driven by selfishness and will
that had distorted his sense of time,
as to how long it took to iron his shirt,
cook the rice for his meals,
or fill the tub for his bath.

However much love overcomes
pity, there is an overshadowing penalty.
Love slackens in its flow,
like that of slack water,
and turns, in tidal memory,
toward indifference,
the forgetting of what had been good.

Ann:

Since it was the last month of the *renshi*, I hoped for a title that would permit me to thank everyone. I'm glad I could take the phrase, "what had been," from the last line of Juliet's poem. I wanted to acknowledge not only writers and publishers but everyone who supports literature, including all who work in schools, libraries, and those who recommend and read literature. Due to everyone, stories are available for the next generation to experience.

I appreciate being a part of this *renshi*. Working with a community of poets throughout the year is a rare experience, and I'm glad I had this opportunity. Mahalo, Juliet, Jean, Christy, Darrell, Eric, Marie, Wing Tek, Sammie, Jason, and everyone who helped.

> **What Had Been**
>
> Listen to language
> centuries old
> and from decades past.
>
> Sounds were written in journals,
> archived in libraries, schools, and homes.
>
> My regards to all
> who work in this endeavor
> recording moments
> reading memories
> printing time across the page
>
> finding ways to translate the essence
> of the past
> of the present
> while keeping music intact
> so others will learn
>
> long after we die
> and fade into the pages.

Christy:

I felt a pressure to make a great final poem as this would be the last poem of the project. Perhaps a way to summarize things or the process. It put an enormous amount of pressure on me. Then, with great fortune, Juliet decided not to write a "summary" or "closing" poem. Whew! I could write whatever came up genuinely although it did not come easily at all. In fact this was another eleventh hour poem. It was made in dedication to a friend whose father was passing. In those moments, words can be useless, fleeting, unavailable. Yet, from my heart this sprang up, and as it discusses a fading, as well as a passing of the torch, I thought it very fitting to be the last poem of our year together. My friend has never seen this poem, though, perhaps one day.

As I reflect now on this wonderful opportunity given to me by Darrell Lum, on being a part of this project, I am a bit sad. I looked forward to the new poems weekly and although I am not crazy about every poem I wrote, I believe some are very solid, with a depth and originality born from this process. These poems would never have seen the light of day had it not been for this project or the voices of the women that preceded me each month with their perspectives and art. My deepest gratitude to Jean, Juliet, and Ann—for letting this "young pup" tag along for the ride. I would do it again in a heartbeat.

Fade

If I could give to you your father whole,
but I cannot give to you your father whole,
he would be free of the demons that made him
eat straight from jelly jars then
turned him into a poltergeist
shuffling through the hallways at midnight.
He would be free of the strokes, tics, and tremors
that now reside as unwelcome guests
disregarding the hour.
I would give him to you
firm and familiar like the sinewy
muscles in your arms heavy
with the wisdom gained
by a lifetime spent loving one woman,
the small triumphs,
the shifting joys.
Each memory recalled of a first—

smile, step, word, kiss would be a black strand
on his head till he stood before you
a lush young man, a reflection in the mirror
shining with joy whispering
You are the common ground now, son,
you are my ladder
A blessing that one day you will give
to your own son. You would not
fear the road ahead, you would not
fear words like Alzheimer's, or cancer
or any other dark god disguised
in medical terms.
You would not shield your eyes
as he fades from view
flashing over the horizon.

No Choice but to Follow:
On Linked Poetry

Those of us bred on Western poetry which values the genius of the individual, the creativity of the unique voice, and other romantic notions such as these may find it hard to appreciate poetry in which connections are the part most prized. In order to better understand where *No Choice but to Follow* fits in we need to see how it connects with the linked poetry of Japan.[1]

The variations of Japanese linked poetry, *renga, renku, renshi,* all have the *ren* 連 in common. That's the key to understanding it. *Ren* refers to connecting, as in making contact or being joined, hence, "linked poetry." This kind of poetry has also been called "collaborative" because a group of poets work together to create the whole. So the *ren* is not only about the joining of poems but also the joining of poets.

Renga 連歌, classical Japanese linked poetry, was very popular between the fourteenth and nineteenth centuries and *renku* 連句—short for *haikai no renga* 俳諧之連歌—had its heyday during the Tokugawa period (1615-1868). Surprisingly you can still find *renku* and even some *renga* poetry sites on the Internet today.[2] The modern version, *renshi* 連詩, refers to linked free verse. So the characters for *ga* or *ka* 歌, *ku* 句, and *shi* 詩, all indicate poetry.

Though different, *renga* and *renku* are essentially the same. Both are based on Japan's more than a thousand-year-old tradition of *waka* 和歌 (also known as tanka 短歌), which was once considered the only literary art form worthy of the name. It provided the images, the themes, the words to express Japanese sensibility. In addition, the different parts of *waka* —three lines of 17 syllables (5-7-5, this part was later known as *haiku* 俳句) followed by two lines of 14 syllables (7-7)—are the two types of links in *renga* and *renku*. To write these links four or more poets gathered together, each composing in turn a three-line link followed by a two-line link in a series of one hundred, thirty-six, or eighteen links. Though rare, a *renga* of a thousand links was possible in the past. Poets of *renga* preferred the sequence of a hundred links, while the *renku* poets favored the sequence of thirty-six links. Aside from this difference *renku* differed from *renga* mostly because of its liberated diction. Unlike *renga* and *waka*, *renku* permitted the use of Chinese origin words and compound terms, hence the possibility for abstractions. This led to the inclusion of the names of concrete objects, which some purists considered "low art." However, Bashō (1644-1694) proved that *renku* could be as possessed of heart as *renga*. Through his influence *renku* became a witty and sometimes earthy version of the rather staid *renga*, a kind of common man's reaction to an aristocratic practice.

Earl Miner repeats throughout *Japanese Linked Poetry* that this poetry is a sequential art, which cannot truly be appreciated unless readers consider the totality of the chain instead of specific links. Linked poetry is not composed of a solitary voice telling a single narrative; instead, multiple voices combine to make patterns emerge as a consequence of the rules of sequence.

It was only the first poet who had any freedom of expression in the initial verse called the *hokku* 発句. All succeeding verses were governed by rules that precluded individuality and themes, since "each of the 99 verses [were] composed in response to the conditions set by the previous voice."[3] The poets that followed in rotation had no choice—thus no freedom—except to follow the one who preceded directly and to conform to the rules. Each poem of five lines could thus be read in two ways. I provide the first four links of the Bashō-led *renku* known as "Even the Kite's Feathers":[4]

1. Even the kite's feathers
   have been tidied by the passing shower
   of early winter rain
2. stirred about by a gust of wind
   the withered leaves grow still again
3. from morning onward
   his trousers have been wetted
   in crossing streams
4. and he sees the bamboo bow
   set to frighten badgers off

The poem would be read like this: Link 1, the *hokku*, can stand alone (thus, later it developed into the stand alone haiku); link 1 and 2 form a whole poem; link 2 and 3 another poem; and link 3 and 4 another; and so forth until the end of the sequence. Because the links connected to the preceding and the succeeding link to make up a five-line poem, each link changed in character as the *renga* or *renku* built up.

The changes from one link to another were somewhat determined by the numerous rules imposed which assured variety and surprise. These rules are too arcane for an amateur like me to do them any justice, but an explanation of where images were to be placed on a sheet of paper can help give a hint of this complexity. Knowing that a specific image had to fall on a certain page concretized the rules that deployed images in certain sequences. In order to understand this, it is necessary to consider the paper on which each link would be written.

Typically four sheets of poetry paper were used to record *renga*'s usual hundred verses. (Of course, *renku* had fewer sheets of paper.) The first and last pages held eight links on one side and fourteen on the other (forty-four verses in all); the middle two sheets held fourteen links on each side (fifty-six for a total of hundred). Each sheet of paper had to include the word "flower" and each side, the word "moon." This distribution was required by the rule that says a hundred-verse *renga* must have four "blossom verses" (one for each sheet of paper) and eight "moon verses" (two for each sheet). Words associated with moon were acceptable substitutes. But the name of a flower could not be substituted for the word "flower." There were rules governing the appearance of different phenomena, how many, at what intervals, and in which form of the word.

Such requirements left little room for choice, especially when the links were composed of either seventeen syllables in three lines or fourteen syllables in two lines! Miraculously, though, there is said to emerge a "hidden order" in the sequence of each link, the discovery of which is the source of pleasure for its participants.[5]

Imbued with their poetic tradition, poets knew the associations that clung to certain phrases and images, which ones were strong and which weak. It was this balance of strong and weak, vivid and pale that was sought by the rules.

It was the emerging pattern of images linking past and present within the totality that distinguished the ordinary chain from the extraordinary one.

While in Western tradition the poet fears the label "unoriginal" and tries to avoid repeating images of past poems, the poets of *renga* and *renku* sought to acknowledge the richness of their poetic past through echoes of other voices in their own verses. They were encouraged to think of this poetic past as a "poetic feast" or "poetic banquet" as indicated by the word *utage* 宴.[6]

It was this poetic banquet that Makoto Ooka wanted to share with the young poets of the 1970s. He observed that the technological era had exacerbated a "modern sense of impermanence" which "expressed itself on the one hand as enervation, and on the other as aggressive egocentrism which rejected tradition and norms. It is difficult for people with such ideas to pay heed to the cultural legacies of preceding generations."[7]

Sensing this disconnect from Japan's rich literary history, he embarked on a campaign to propagate *renshi* in Japan and around the world as a means to promote mutual understanding and exchange. Through his encounters with poets of other countries he discovered a keen interest in collaborative creation. While not commonly practiced in Europe today there is a history of collaborative poetry with such forms as the French *tenson*, practiced by troubadours of the Middle Ages.[8] One could describe this writing as a poetic tournament. A poet would express an opinion on a certain topic, inviting others to do the same. The responding poets would, however, take the opposite point of view on the same topic. I guess that's how the French collaborate! The collaboration appears only in the use of the same form: the poets would repeat the same rhyme scheme and engage in debates on love and ethics. One famous exchange occurred between the royal blood, Charles d'Orleans (1394-1465), and the criminal poet, François Villon (1431-1463), the poet of "Where are the snows of yesteryear?" fame, whose name evokes nostalgia for French people. Villon won the tournament with a memorable poem, which begins with "I die of thirst before this fountain." Variations of the *tenson* also existed in other European countries.

I digress only to illustrate that collaborative poetry was not foreign in Europe, which in part explains Ooka's success in arranging linked poetry sessions in Berlin, Rotterdam, Paris, Helsinki, Frankfort, and Lahti (Finland). Another example is the event arranged in 1969 by Octavio Paz. He and three other poets created their own kind of renga in Paris ten years before the official appearance of the word *renshi*.[9] Paz conducted a quadrilingual experiment with Charles Tomlinson (English), Jacques Roubaud (French), Edoardo Sanguineti (Italian), and himself (Spanish). In imitation of the Japanese model, they linked the four parts of a sonnet using the two quatrains-two tercets form. Each wrote in his own language. So the first quatrain was in French, the next in English, the first tercet in Italian and the second in Spanish. It was a kind of a linguistic clamor. The whole thing was translated into these different languages and published in 1971 as *Renga*.[10]

Ooka attributes the West's familiarity with the word *renga* to Paz's experiment.[11] He perceptively points out how the shock of this public display of poetry writing had an unsettling effect on these Western poets. Since poets traditionally wrote *renga* in each other's presence, Paz and his cohorts gathered in a French hotel and wrote. Paz confessed: "I write in front of others, the others in front of me. Something like undressing in a cafe, or defecating, crying before strangers. The Japanese invented the *renga* for the same reasons and in the same manner in which they bathed naked in public."[12] Ooka comments, "This confession vividly shows just how far the new experience of collective creation dragged the poet from his ordinary sensibility, and it is extremely interesting despite the fact that the Japanese did not actually invent *renga* in the same way that they strip naked in the public bath-houses!"[13]

You might have gathered from our commentaries that we *No Choice but to Follow*-poets did feel at times like we were stripping naked in the bathhouse. Once written, our poems were immediately displayed for the world to see on the Bamboo Ridge Press website. We didn't have the cover of edit to erase the *faux pas*; we didn't have the friendly suggestion to correct an infelicity. Paz and his poets, though writing face to face, did not expose themselves to the world until later, after corrections could be made. Wing

Tek tells me that he and other readers waited in anticipation for our links, feeling the excitement of the reveal. As we stripped off each week, these eyes participated in our collaborative effort.[14] We became a collective. Although, in the 1970s, Ooka saw technology as exacerbating a disconnected world, the Internet has created a means of instant interconnectedness. Poets and readers can participate in the process. On the Bamboo Ridge website, readers were invited to comment on the *renshi* as well as post their own poems in a separate "Bamboo Shoots" area.

We also could not hide behind a web of rules because we had but one rule suggested by Ooka to use as a guideline: "a poet takes the last line or last word of the previous poet written by another as the title of his own poem. In thus capping the previous poem, the poet has some sense of continuity or of expanding or developing its ideas, but in a very different direction."[15] Juliet's lyrical expanses into memory and reflection cannot be confused with the muscle of my verses or with Ann's terse tenderness. Christy's desire not to repeat herself or imitate us causes her to explore different possibilities including dance, the contemplation of art, and the growing of tumors!

We each have a distinct voice, which somehow miraculously sings a unique song. We broke a *renga* taboo in November by having a theme, when we wrote of President Obama. But how could we avoid mulling over the election in November 2008, when the fate of our country was ever present on our mind?

We poets did not yet have a shared past, but the process of the year did create a past for us, a connection which continues to hold us together today. The writing of this book and the events that will ensue will no doubt solidify our community, and we will fondly remember how we sweated out each word, dreaded each deadline and sometimes marveled at the result of our collective effort, no doubt grateful for these poems, which would never have been written without *renshi*. We are also pleased, I think, to be part of a revival of interest in collaborative poetry.

One could say that today's poetry slams, while not exactly collaborative, represent the communal and competitive side of poetry. I should not leave you with the impression that there was no competition involved in the writing of Japanese linked poetry. Of course, there was. Poets would challenge their opponents to better show off their prowess. "The more absurd or puzzling the content of the first man's lines, the greater the achievement of the second man if he managed to add two or three lines that, perhaps by a clever play on words, made sense of the whole."[16]

We hope that through our year's worth of links a sense of the whole has emerged, and that the pleasure derived from *No Choice but to Follow* is the satisfaction of *utage*, truly a poetic feast!

☙

[1] I am not a specialist of linked poetry or of Japanese literature for that matter. I offer my comments here primarily as a dilettante who has participated in several *renshi* events and read about the subject, mostly articles written by Makoto Ooka. Anyone interested in learning more about linked poetry should start with Earl Miner's *Japanese Linked Poetry* (New Jersey: Princeton University Press, 1979). Hereafter cited as Miner. Another more recent addition to this area of study is Esperanza Ramirez-Christensen's *Emptiness and Temporality: Buddhism and Medieval Japanese Poetics* (Stanford University Press, 2008). She explains that a *renga* is like "a miniature *waka* anthology." Having given this caution, I take full responsibility for my words.

[2] A good place to start are the links in Wikipedia: http://en.wikipedia.org/wiki/Renga.

[3] Konishi Jin'ichi's, "The Art of Renga," translated with an introduction by Karen Brazell and Lewis Cook, *The Journal of Japanese Studies* 2:1 (Autumn, 1975): 37. This article provides a very good overview of the complexity of *renga*. Hereafter cited as Konishi.

[4] Translated in Miner p. 282

[5] Konishi p. 48

[6] Ooka Makoto, "Renga—Linked Poems," in *A Play of Mirrors: Eight Major Poets of Modern Japan*, ed. by Ooka Makoto and Thomas Fitzsimmons

(Rochester: Katydid Books, Oakland University, 1987), p. 201. Hereafter cited as *Mirrors*.

7 "Linked Poetry: Experiments with Western Poets," which appeared in *Acta Asiatica* 56, "Continuity and Discontinuity in Japanese Literature," (Tokyo: The Tōhō Gakkai, 1989) p. 97. Hereafter cited as *Acta Asiatica*.

8 I thank Bill Burgwinkle, a former colleague, now teaching at Cambridge University, who told me about the *tenson*.

9 Ooka recounts that the word "acquired citizenship only after the publication in June, 1979 of *Kai: renshi* 櫂 連詩." He and his fellow poets had gathered together over a period of seven years, writing in free verse in sequences of one to ten lines *Acta Asiatica* p. 90.

10 Octavio Paz, Jacques Roubaud, Edoardo Sanguineti, and Charles Tomlinson, *Renga, A Chain of Poems* (New York: George Braziller, 1971). Henceforth cited as Paz.

11 *Acta Asiatica* p. 93.

12 Paz p. 22.

13 *Mirrors*, p. 205.

14 It was Wing Tek who explained this to me but not with the same metaphor.

15 Makoto Ooka in *What the Kite Thinks* along with Wing Tek Lum, Joseph Stanton, Jean Yamasaki Toyama, edited by Lucy Lower (Honolulu: University of Hawai'i, 1994), p. 46.

16 Donald Keene explains this in *World Within Walls: Japanese literature of the pre-modern era 1600-1867* (New York: Holt, Rinehart and Winston, 1976) p. 11.

ABOUT THE POETS

Ann Inoshita was born and raised on Oʻahu. She has published poems in *Bamboo Ridge*, *Hawaiʻi Pacific Review*, *Hawaiʻi Review*, and *Tinfish*. Her book of poems, *Mānoa Stream*, was published by Kahuaomānoa Press in 2007. Her short play, *Wea I Stay: A Play in Hawaiʻi*, was included in *The Statehood Project*, performed by Kumu Kahua Theatre and published by Fat Ulu Productions. She has an M.A. in English from the University of Hawaiʻi at Mānoa and currently teaches at Kapiʻolani Community College.

Most recently, **Juliet S. Kono** has been featured in *Imagine What It's Like*, an anthology which combines literature and medicine. Forthcoming is *Anshuu: Dark Sorrow*, a historical novel set in Hawaiʻi and Japan, which will be published in 2010. Born and raised in Hilo, Hawaiʻi, she lives in Honolulu with her husband and continues to teach at Leeward Community College. She received her Jodo Shinshu Tokudo (entrance into the priesthood) ordination in 2007 and works toward reflecting the Dharma reality in her daily life.

Born and raised on the island of Oʻahu, **Christy Passion** has, in recent years, been drawn to both poetry and short story writing. Her work has been published in local venues such as *Bamboo Ridge*, *Hawaiʻi Pacific Review*, and the anthology *Honolulu Stories*. Her poetry has won both local and national awards, including the James Vaughn Award, The Atlanta Review International Merit Award, and the Academy of American Poetry Award. She works as a critical care nurse at the Queen's Medical Center. This is her first book.

Jean Yamasaki Toyama is a poet, scholar, translator, and writer of fiction. She is emerita professor of French at the University of Hawaiʻi at Mānoa, where she taught and was associate dean of the College of Languages, Linguistics and Literature. She lives in Hawaiʻi where she was born and raised.

CD PLAYLIST

Track	Poem	Poet	Page	Time
1	How Does Bamboo Ridge	Jean Yamasaki Toyama	23	0:46
2	Plug Along	Juliet S. Kono	24	1:01
3	The Next Life	Ann Inoshita	25	0:34
4	Into the Wild	Christy Passion	26	1:03
5	No Choice but to Follow	Jean Yamasaki Toyama	27	0:29
6	He Just Had to Make Sure	Juliet S. Kono	28	0:47
7	What Will Become of Them?	Ann Inoshita	29	0:27
8	Breathe; a seduction	Christy Passion	30	0:47
9	Jalousied Window	Jean Yamasaki Toyama	31	0:32
10	Coming Home	Juliet S. Kono	32	0:49
11	Embrace	Ann Inoshita	33	0:21
12	One Page	Christy Passion	34	1:18
13	Faithless, without Memory	Jean Yamasaki Toyama	35	1:08
14	Of Our Remembrances	Juliet S. Kono	37	1:18
15	My Memory of Your Eyes	Ann Inoshita	39	0:37
16	Smile in the Wind	Christy Passion	40	1:38
17	He Feels His Tumor Grow	Jean Yamasaki Toyama	42	0:51
18	All That Unknowing	Juliet S. Kono	43	1:31
19	Shattered Water	Ann Inoshita	45	0:40
20	Hear the Dogs Crying	Christy Passion	46	1:30
21	Do You Know My Name?	Jean Yamasaki Toyama	48	0:59
22	Face Looking from the Mirror	Juliet S. Kono	49	0:46
23	Before She Leaves	Ann Inoshita	50	0:26
24	From the Clouds	Christy Passion	51	1:26
25	From this Darkness	Jean Yamasaki Toyama	53	0:51
26	Buzzing Along with Us	Juliet S. Kono	54	1:46
27	Without Meaning to Be Cruel	Ann Inoshita	56	1:59
28	She Asked	Christy Passion	58	0:42
29	All We Do Not Know	Jean Yamasaki Toyama	59	1:08
30	Of the Whys and Wherefores	Juliet S. Kono	60	1:14
31	We're Here	Ann Inoshita	62	0:37
32	It Was Morning	Christy Passion	63	1:33
33	Canvas	Jean Yamasaki Toyama	65	1:07
34	It Was Like Finding Gold	Juliet S. Kono	66	1:02
35	The Uncreated	Ann Inoshita	67	0:31
36	The Room Fills with	Christy Passion	68	1:01
37	Trying to Warn Me	Jean Yamasaki Toyama	69	0:35
38	There'll Be Hell to Pay	Juliet S. Kono	70	1:05
39	To Have or Need	Ann Inoshita	71	0:46
40	Depending on Lights to Guide My Way	Christy Passion	72	0:57
41	The Fires	Jean Yamasaki Toyama	73	0:28
42	Let the Great Healing Begin	Juliet S. Kono	74	0:57
43	Shine of Tears	Ann Inoshita	75	0:36
44	Prepare to Move into the White House	Christy Passion	76	1:01
45	Just Enough Shave Ice	Jean Yamasaki Toyama	77	0:43
46	Not Pau Yet	Juliet S. Kono	78	1:04
47	What Had Been	Ann Inoshita	79	0:36
48	Fade	Christy Passion	80	1:14

Total: 45:17